IN THE SCHOOL OF
SAINT BENEDICT

IN THE SCHOOL OF
SAINT BENEDICT

Benedictine Spirituality for Every Christian

DOM XAVIER PERRIN OSB

Abbot of Quarr

GRACEWING

À l'école de saint Benoît, La spiritualité bénédictine à l'usage de tous les chrétiens first published by Editions de l'Emmanuel, 2020.

English translation by Sr Lætitia Payne of St Cecilia's Abbey, Ryde, and Dom Luke Bell of Quarr Abbey, Ryde

First published in England in 2022
by
Graceming
2 Southern Avenue
Leominster
Herefordshire HR6 0QF
United Kingdom
www.gracewing.co.uk

ISBN 9780852449851

Typeset by Gracewing
Cover design by Bernardita Peña Hurtado

Cover photo © mlburguiere

To my fathers and brothers of Kergonan,
united with them in the praise
and love of Christ.

CONTENTS

PREFACE

A QUARTER OF A century ago, when I was a young, somewhat anxious seeker on a vocational quest, keen to find familiar coordinates to steer by, I asked the author of this book if he thought St Benedict was a humanist. Like a good monk, he pondered the question and did not answer at once. The next day he gave a considered reply. No, he told me, he did not think the notion 'humanist' apt. There was too much theory attached to it. He would be more inclined to say, simply, that the Father of Western monasticism had been profoundly *human*. I have always been grateful for that observation.

The monastic life is life lived by supernatural criteria. At the same time it is a radically human life. Indeed, the challenge of owning oneself as oneself, of making peace, not just with humanity in general, but with oneself as a human person, is the first major combat a novice encounters. Anyone who has essayed it knows it can be fierce.

But what peace springs from it, what broad vistas! The realisation that it is possible to abandon pretence and embrace vulnerability, to find oneself carried by a surprising graciousness of mercy made concrete through the brethren, is freeing and joyful. One discovers what potential lies hidden in humanity, even one's own, in all its poverty.

Abbot Xavier's book presents the Benedictine way with clarity born of experience. May it open the eyes of many to the wholesome challenges and great happiness that can be found along this way.

In *A Time to Keep Silence*, first published in 1953, Patrick Leigh Fermor reflected on the strange pull monasticism exercised on him. It was, he wrote, 'deeper than mere interest and curiosity, and more important than the pleasure an historian or an aesthete finds in ancient buildings and liturgy'. In this life which, at first, from afar, had seemed alien, he found something reassuring and familiar. He discovered important truths about himself.

The monastic, Benedictine heritage has precious gifts to offer a time in which many are perplexed about what it means to be human. Thank God there are, even now, trustworthy guides around to introduce this humane school of life with authority, attractively.

+FR ERIK VARDEN OCSO
Bishop-Prelate of the Prelature of Trondheim

INTRODUCTION

Saint Benedict, Master of the Christian Life

TO PRESENT SAINT Benedict as a master of Christian spirituality is both obvious and yet something of a challenge.

On the one hand, no one would dream of denying the role monasteries living under the *Rule* of St Benedict have played, and continue to play, in the spiritual life of Christians. People instinctively realise that monks and nuns are a hidden presence of adoration and intercession upholding the lives of all their Christian brothers and sisters. We often like to express this dimension of the Church's life by referring to the image of Moses praying on the mountain while Israel was fighting down on the plain (cf. Ex 17: 8–16). Just as the soldiers' success depended on Moses' perseverance in prayer, in the same way the fidelity of Christians is directly linked to the silent combat of those who stand, day and night and for their whole lives, turned towards God.

Nevertheless, Saint Benedict wrote for monasteries and not for people living in the world. The central values of his spiritual message—such as obedience, silence and humility—thus need to be transposed, even translated, in order to be applicable in an ordinary Christian life. The faithful lay person who wants to be inspired by Saint Benedict in his or her daily life must take up the challenge represented by this adaptation.

Let us state at once that he or she will be helped by Saint Benedict himself, and first of all by the Patriarch of monks' realism. Just as he knows how to be clear and uncompromising when defining his objectives, he is equally flexible when it comes to the means to be used. His eminently practical genius gives him a great understanding of the landscape, enabling him to rapidly evaluate its possibilities as well as its limits. He constantly adapts himself to places and circumstances, and above all to people.

His realism—his profound "Yes" to the reality of human existence—finds its source in the contemplation of the mystery of the Incarnation. For Saint Benedict, "Nothing must be preferred to Christ", whom he lovingly considers in the truth of His Incarnation, the humility of His Passion, and the glory of His eternal Kingdom with the Father. In this way, Saint Benedict constantly brings his disciples back to the heart of the life of faith: the Person of the Word Incarnate. Considered from this angle, it becomes clear that the monastic life is substantially the same as the Christian life. It consists in opening oneself up as much as possible to Christ, following Him obediently and imitating Him in all humility, in order to begin participating in the treasury of Divine Love contained in His Heart. Here, Benedictine spirituality returns to the same hearth wherein all spiritualities meet and harmonise: Christ, who is the Church's life, the life of every Christian as of every monk.

The following pages are intended to help us discover the person and teaching of Saint Benedict (Chapter 1), to give a glimpse of the richness and relevance of his spiritual heritage throughout the centuries (Chapter 2), and to suggest some ways in which we can begin to make our own what is most essentially Christian in the Benedictine monastic charism (Chapter 3).

Quarr Abbey
21 March 2020
Feast of the Transitus of our Holy Father Saint Benedict

1 MEETING SAINT BENEDICT

I T IS IMPOSSIBLE to live in Western Europe without
encountering the figure of Saint Benedict of Nursia
(480–547), the Patriarch of western monks. Towns
and provinces are dotted with reminiscences of a monastic
past, architectural remains or simple place names. In
England, Canterbury, Westminster, York Minster, Win-
chester and Worcester Cathedrals all grew up alongside
Benedictine monasteries and famous abbeys flourished at
Romsey, Bury St Edmunds, Bath and Rievaulx, to mention
but a few. The list of these cloisters for both men and
women, reminding us of Saint Benedict's presence, is
endless. Furthermore, if you are consulting an ancient
manuscript, in the Bodleian for example, you will often
find that it comes from an abbey suppressed at the
Reformation. If you are you interested in the early history
of a parish church or village chapel, more than once you
will discover that it has a monastic origin. Historians tell
us that there was an "age of monks" in Western Europe.
It extends over a long period from the end of the Roman
Empire, in about the 6th Century, as far as the establishment of towns and cities and the modern State from the
13th Century onwards. This epoch has left impressive
traces. In a way, for those who know how to look, Benedict
and his followers are present everywhere, as a discreet
reminder of the period when they provided the framework
for the formation of Christian European civilization.

This omnipresence of Benedict renders all the more
paradoxical his own relatively elusive identity. In fact, it is
not so easy to approach the man who stands behind the

many monuments built by his disciples in the course of the centuries. He is known to us principally through two texts: the *Rule for Monks*, which he wrote around 530 (henceforth abbreviated to *Rule* or RB followed by the number of the chapter and then the number of the verse), and the account *The Life and Miracles of Saint Benedict of Nursia,* composed by Pope Saint Gregory the Great around 594 as the second book of his *Dialogues* (henceforth abbreviated to *Life*). The former is a short legislative text which continues to regulate the life of thousands of monasteries of men and of women, Benedictine and Cistercian, throughout the world. Although St Gregory's narrative is our principal source for the main stages of Saint Benedict's life, it cannot be considered a biography in the modern sense of the word. Its purpose is moral rather than historical. The author seeks to edify by means of a pleasant tale wherein the wonderful plays a major role. He is certainly relying on eye witnesses and is recounting events whose authenticity he has ascertained, but neither chronological precision nor the psychology of his hero are among his primary preoccupations. He is not painting a portrait, he is writing an icon, and God's light fascinates him even more than the individual who is filled with that light. Such as it is, however, this text can still provide us with the principal stages in Saint Benedict's itinerary.

Saint Benedict at Subiaco

About the year 500, a young student leaves Rome and reaches the mountains situated south west of the capital, not far from Tivoli. He has already left his family, who live in Nursia, a hundred and sixty kilometres north of Rome. He gives up the intellectual formation which his parents' wealth has made available to him. He flees a harmful moral atmosphere, thirsty for solitude, silence and renunciation. Above all, he is fascinated by God and wishes to consecrate himself entirely to His service. Because of Him, he flees the world. Italy at the very beginning of the 6th Century is not a country at peace. What still remains of the institutions inherited from the Roman Empire is constantly being undermined by the attacks of the invading barbarians. No one feels safe, there is always the risk of being attacked by more or less violent hordes who sack the towns and pillage the countryside. This leads to famines, with all their associated miseries.

Benedict withdraws from this troubled world. Like so many others before him, he sets off in search of God and the peace which God gives. He goes deep into the desert. Since the 3rd Century, men and women in relatively large numbers have done the same and this marks the beginning of monasticism. The monk withdraws. He separates himself from the world and its moral corruption in order to lead a life placed under the sign of God's light and the grace of the Gospel. Far from the cities, where Christianity has known its first developments, this man with his passion for the absolute goes into the desert to search for a life free from all compromise. He is searching for God and, in order to reach Him, he strips himself of everything. He renounces his possessions and his affections, and he makes himself a disciple of the Holy Spirit, who guides him by the ways of the Gospel and by the examples of tradition.

On his way, Benedict meets the monk Romanus who lives in a nearby monastery. He understands what the young runaway is looking for. He gives him the monastic habit and promises to support him discreetly. It is appropriate to underline that Benedict does not invent monasticism. Rather he inserts himself into a living tradition that is already ancient in his time. He makes his way through

its stages in an exceptional way. Above all, he understands
and is able to give expression to its spirit and institutions
with all the clarity of a true master. But he is not a founding
father doing something completely original. He makes the
monastic charism his own, and his special gift is to do this
in such a way that his *Rule* will become an essential link
in the chain of its transmission.

The first period of Benedict's life at Subiaco is lived in
solitude. There he leads a very austere life; we can guess
that it alternates, as has become traditional since the Desert
Fathers in Egypt, between prayer, reading the word of God
and manual labour. From the very beginning, his undertaking is opposed by the one Saint Gregory the Great calls "the
old enemy". One aspect of life in the desert is precisely this
combat with the devil, following the example given by Jesus
after his baptism by John in the Jordan, when he withdrew
into solitude for forty days. If Rome is overflowing with
temptations, Subiaco is characterised by the presence of
the Tempter who comes forward, as it were, with his face
unveiled. The desert, then, is not only the place of rest
where a soul may give itself up to the joys of contemplation.
It is first of all the arena for an arduous combat. Whoever
goes in search of God encounters all the ways in which he
collaborates with sin. The solitary needs good psychological
equilibrium and genuine interior strength in order to stand
firm in the midst of the tensions which accompany the
struggle between what Saint Paul calls the "flesh" and the
"Spirit" (cf. Gal 5). Benedict stands firm, and soon, Saint
Gregory tells us, God begins to make his virtue known to
other men, first a priest who visits him on Easter day. The
hermit, in his separation from the world, did not know the
exact date of the feast. He learns it with joy. The two men
then exchange spiritual reflections before sharing a festive
meal and giving thanks. Let us notice this Easter grace in

Saint Benedict's life: it is on the day of the celebration of the central mystery of the Christian faith that Benedict leaves the permanent Lent into which he had resolutely plunged himself, and that he enters into the light of fraternal communion. A little while afterwards, some shepherds fortuitously come across him. They soon benefit from his exhortations to accept the Gospel.

The hermit's reputation grows. Then the monks of a nearby monastery choose him as their superior. He agrees, not without hesitation, and immediately begins to inaugurate strict discipline. The community is soon sorry to have called upon this zealot and sets about getting rid of him by poisoning his portion of wine. Benedict makes the usual gesture of blessing and immediately the carafe shatters. Benedict understands everything. Perfectly composed, he stands up and informs the monks that he is leaving them. So he returns to his beloved solitude, to live there under the gaze of God alone. This incident speaks volumes about the tepidity and mediocrity that is always ready to undermine monastic communities; it likewise reveals that Saint Benedict's sanctity could perhaps still be rather rigid. This dialectic between the absolute of the search for perfection and the mediocrity lived by most men lies at the heart of the *Rule*'s equilibrium. In his mature years, Saint Benedict will find a way of preserving the purity of the ideal while showing himself understanding towards the weaknesses of individuals. This equilibrium between rigour and moderation will become a distinctive characteristic of the Benedictine spirit.

For the time being, Benedict immerses himself again in being alone with God, but only to be soon joined by very many disciples. It is not his mission to restore an existing monastery, but to begin a new branch on the monastic tree. Saint Gregory speaks of his establishing twelve

monasteries around Subiaco. It is probably a matter of
semi-independent houses where the monks live in small
communities, all having a relationship with the central
person of the spiritual father, who remains their superior
and their master. Youths and children are entrusted to
Benedict's care in order to receive an education. Schools,
as well as missionary activities, can claim to be following
the example of Benedict himself, and have not failed to
develop over the centuries.

St Gregory's account continues with various miracle
stories, which reveal to us a wonder-working Benedict, but
especially a man with a gift for discerning spirits. Soon,
however, a priest in the area proves jealous of him and
begins to persecute Benedict and his disciples. The holy
abbot sees in this a sign that he must leave for another
place. He nominates superiors for all the monasteries he
has founded and, followed by a nucleus of disciples, goes
away again, probably about the year 530.

At Monte Cassino

His travels lead him further south of Rome to the site of
Monte Cassino—an elevated plateau dominating a large
plain. The area is even more out of the way, and a lively
form of paganism is still practised there. Benedict destroys
a temple and cuts down a sacred grove in order to build
his monastery. This time the community is all together in
one place. The buildings are bigger. The life of this larger
group is also more unified by the observance of a more
precise rule. It is during this period of his life (530–547
according to the generally accepted dates) that Benedict
writes his *Rule* for monks. From the cave where he lived
as a hermit, he has moved on to what the eastern monks
called a *lavra*, namely an informal group of disciples

gathered round a spiritual master. We find him now at the head of a well-organised monastery, ordered by obedience to the abbot and the celebration in common of the liturgical hours of prayer. The holy pope then shows us a Benedict who has arrived at the summit of his saintly life. He raises the dead, reads hearts, foretells the future, makes oil abound in a time of famine, reconciles the dead with God and reprehends the powerful of this world. Behind all these miraculous signs, Saint Gregory allows us to glimpse a man of great faith, deeply humble, full of confidence in God's help, convinced of the goodness, but also the severity of the Almighty. We can make out a strong personality, a temperament readily demanding of himself and authoritative towards others, a man whom life has led along a path of conversion towards patience, gentleness and mercy. The fire which burned in the heart of the young hermit is still there, ready to flash forth in holy anger when he meets pride, dishonesty, murmuring or disobedience with regard to the common rule. But henceforth he is filled with a richness of profound charity, full of humanity and radiating peace. Under his leadership, the monastery situated on the mountain becomes radiant. The villages round about are evangelised. The bishops and clergy of the area find light and friendship in the man of God. Benedictine monasticism is born.

The final phase of Saint Gregory's account allows us to perceive something of Saint Benedict's mystical life. In the episode of the meeting with his sister, Saint Scholastica, the love of God and the desire for heaven take precedence over the strict observance of the rule, for the greater joy of the brother and sister. The nocturnal vision of the whole world caught up in the light of God represents a summit of the contemplative life. From then on, Benedict sees the world as God sees it, in that light and love which make it appear at one and the same time so little and so important. The holy abbot's life can draw to a close. He foretells his death to his disciples, has his tomb prepared, and after a week's illness, asks to be carried to the oratory of the monastery, where he receives the Eucharist as viaticum. He dies standing in prayer, surrounded by his own, on 21 March 547, according to the generally accepted date. The miracles that accompany the announcement of his death, and which flower in the places where he had lived, confirm his sanctity. Thus concludes Saint Gregory's account.

This brief summary does not exempt us from reading the papal biographer's beautiful text, which teems with very interesting spiritual insights, while being written with elegance and sprinkled with perceptive details full of fine humour. The portrait that is drawn as the chapters succeed one another allows us to glimpse St Benedict's itinerary. The hermit, who had sacrificed everything for God alone and chosen to be unknown by the world, has been led by God to become the spiritual master of many disciples. For them, he has built monasteries. He has untiringly lavished his teaching upon them, both by his word and by his example. Finally, he has drawn up for them a rule full of wisdom. Very soon, Benedict has ceased to belong to himself. His life has been dedicated to the service of souls: those of the monks first of all, but also, those of the children entrusted to the monastery for their education, those of guests and pilgrims, especially the poorest, those of the clergy and people round about. This intense activity has not prevented him from maintaining a great intimacy with the Lord, nourished by liturgical and personal prayer, by regular reading of the word of God, and by spiritual and mystical conversations with some individuals close to him. Benedict has grown in every aspect, becoming ever more open to God and more welcoming towards those who, in ever greater numbers, have recourse to him in their most varied needs. He ends his life in a Eucharistic communion which seals his whole existence, his passing through death and his entry into life, with the seal of the love of Christ, and makes of it a gift to the Church of every age. He stands as a living icon of the praise of God and of universal communion in His love.

The Rule for Monks

"He wrote a rule for monks, remarkable for its discretion and agreeable style. Anyone who wants to know what he was like and how he lived will be able to discover all of this in the precepts of this rule. For the man of God did not teach other than as he lived."[1] Saint Gregory himself refers his readers to the *Rule* in order for them to find out more about Saint Benedict, and it is true that his Rule reveals him to us even better than the *Life*. Perhaps the saintly pope's recommendation—he was one of the most widely read authors in the West in the Middle Ages—had a role to play in the attention given to the *Rule* in the monastic environ- ments that would progressively come to adopt it as their unique text of reference. Nevertheless, the *Rule*'s intrinsic qualities are sufficient recommendation in themselves.

When Benedict writes his *Rule*, he takes his place in the line of those who have legislated for the monastic world before him. Among them we must note Saint Pachomius and Saint Basil, in the East. In the Latin world, we encoun- ter the *Rule of Saint Augustine* written at the very end of the 4th Century, as well as the *Rules of the Fathers* coming from the monastic milieu of Lérins and Agaune in the following decades. Above all, a rule written in Italy in the first half of the 5th Century, whose author is unknown and

---

[1]   *Life*, ch. 36.

which has been handed down to us under the title of *The Rule of the Master*, is a direct source for Benedict. He has drawn abundantly from this, retaining with great freedom what suited him and unhesitatingly leaving aside almost two thirds of the text. Alongside these monastic rules, which Saint Benedict knew at least in part (he seems only to have had access to an incomplete Latin translation of the *Rules* of St. Basil), there is the whole corpus of monastic literature with which Benedict is familiar. He has read translations of the sayings and lives of the Egyptian Desert Fathers. He is familiar with the *Conferences* and *Institutes* of John Cassian—two major works with regard to the transmission in the West of the monastic teaching of the East. He has drawn more than one inspiration from Saint Augustine. The monastic texts of Saint Jerome and of Rufinus of Aquileia are not unfamiliar to him. Moreover, he readily refers to this monastic library, making no claims to originality. He wants to be part of an authentic tradition, while recognising the need to reformulate this in response to the realities he sees, to the men he encounters, and the challenges it seems to him he has to engage with.

The *Rule* is, after the Bible, the text witnessed by the highest number of medieval manuscripts[2], testifying to its

---

2   Two manuscripts in particular deserve our attention. The Bodleian library in Oxford preserves the oldest redaction of the *Rule*, dating from the first decade of the 8th Century. The library of the Abbey of St Gall, in Switzerland, contains a manuscript brought there in 841 from the Abbey of Reichenau by the monk Grimald, which specialists recognise as a copy made in 817 of the text which Paul the Deacon had himself copied in Rome in 787, at the request of Charlemagne. These two venerable documents testify to two slightly different versions of the text of the *Rule*. Experts generally recognise that the "long text" of the Saint-Gall manuscript is more authoritative, although more recent, and seems to testify to a more ancient tradition.

success and its extraordinary diffusion. In particular, one cannot fail to be struck by the early spread of the *Rule* in English monasteries—perhaps in the wake of the evangelising mission of Saint Augustine of Canterbury in 597—and as far as the Abbey of Saint-Gall in Switzerland, a veritable citadel of monasticism founded by the spiritual sons of the Irish monk Saint Columban (543–615). The communities of the early Middle Ages loved to draw on monastic tradition and did not hesitate to be inspired in their observance by several rules, the most frequently used being those of Saint Columban and Saint Benedict. It was only at the beginning of the second millennium that the *Rule* of Saint Benedict gradually became the sole point of reference for monasteries in the West.

When God calls: the Prologue

The *Rule* is a short text consisting of seventy three chapters, most of them not exceeding just a few paragraphs, preceded by a *Prologue* (henceforth abbreviated to Prologue followed by verse number). In this initial exhortation, Saint Benedict announces the invitation to the monastic life and explains the end he has in view: establishing "a school of the Lord's service", wherein may be taught the way that leads to God and to eternal life. The similarity between this kind of introductory homily and ancient baptismal catecheses has long been recognised. The monastic calling is directly rooted in the grace of baptism. It is wedded to its fundamental movement of conversion. God's voice is addressed to man and exhorts him to turn away from evil in order to return to his Creator. The monk's path imitates the journey of the repentant prodigal son who returns to his father (cf. Lk 15). Their meeting is accompanied by a revelation of the divine mercy which forgives sins and fully restores filial dignity.

This general rule of salvation becomes for the one who is called to monastic life the horizon of his whole existence. The monk is a Christian who simply tries to follow through his baptism fully. The outward forms and particular circumstances of each one's vocation are of less importance than its essential substance: answering the Gospel call, seizing the grace of conversion and salvation offered by the merciful God who invites us to follow Christ into his Heavenly Kingdom. The monastic institution has no other goal but to help us attain this end by guaranteeing our constancy and guiding our efforts in the task of conversion.

So, Saint Benedict describes the monastery as a "school of the Lord's service".[3] In it, a group of disciples share a common life, under the guidance of a spiritual master and with the wisdom of a Rule of Life tested by long experience. The monks thus go forward together toward the full encounter with the God of love revealed in Jesus Christ, an encounter which will also be the accomplishment of their ultimate identity as adopted sons of their Heavenly Father. A truly mystical inspiration runs through the *Prologue*. In discreet but powerful terms, Saint Benedict suggests the intensity of the Divine love which calls, sustains, encourages and stimulates us along the way, before welcoming and crowning us in eternity. The fire of love which burned in the heart of the young hermit of Subiaco runs through these few pages, in which so many men and women throughout the centuries have recognised Christ's call. Undertaking the monastic life is a love adventure calling our hearts to enlarge "with an unutterable sweetness of love".[4]

---

[3]   Prologue 45.
[4]   Prologue 49.

The Monastic Institution

The *Rule* is not composed according to a rigorously strict plan. We can, however, distinguish major sections which will help us grasp its contents. It opens with three chapters in which Saint Benedict delineates his vision of the kind of monastic community for which he is legislating. All sorts of impostors circulate under the name of monk, he warns in the first chapter. Some spend their time boasting about their title as monks in order to be received and honoured everywhere, without taking on any of the demands of the monastic life. Others chose a regime that suits them, gathering in small groups of like-minded men, looking honourable enough, but allowing themselves to become lax. Benedict of course detests both these kinds. On the other hand, he is full of respect and admiration for hermits engaged in solitary combat in the desert. He recommends, however, that these latter be men tested by several years of life in an authentic monastery, and sufficiently trained to face the difficulties proper to the solitary life. In other words, he does not recommend the path he himself took, thereby perhaps recognising its exceptional character. There remain the cenobites, whom he highly esteems and for whom he legislates. As the twofold roots of the Greek from which it is formed suggests, the word "cenobites" designates people who lead the common life.

Life in community, as Benedict envisages it, consists of three essential elements: cenobites, he writes, "live in monasteries, and serve under a rule and an abbot".[5] By "monastery" he understands a true religious house where a serious life is led with perseverance and fidelity. No one there does just whatever pleases him, but everyone follows the precepts of a rule and the guidance of an abbot. The

---

[5]   RB 1,1.

rule fixes the general norms, supplies the framework, describes the fundamental principles, foresees the most frequent situations that may arise, underlines the important things and defines the ways decisions are made and government exercised. It falls to the abbot to put into practice its application, to indicate what is appropriate in particular circumstances, to decide in more delicate situations, in short, to adapt with flexibility and firmness to all the situations of life. This kind of common life, then, is anything but improvised. It is constructed on solid foundations, which are those of the structure of the *monastery*, whose architecture, even if simple, corresponds to the needs of the community living there in a stable way, the *rule* of life, accepted by all, which guarantees the authenticity of the life, and finally the legitimate *superior*, who assures the cohesion of the group and maintains its spiritual dynamism. Starting with this first chapter, we meet the characteristic elements of Benedictine monasticism: a community tending towards communion in fraternal charity and in the praise of God, based on a well-regulated life, and with a fundamental dimension of obedience to the will of God, as manifested by the requirements of the rule and the abbot's discernment.

The Abbot's Spiritual Paternity

The two following chapters, then, focus in turn on the abbot and on the community. In the golden age of early monasticism, those who went out to the Egyptian deserts would place themselves under the tutelage of a spiritual master, whose old Coptic name of *appa* would be handed on in successive translations as *abba, abbas, abbot*. It is very dangerous to launch out alone into the desert in a spiritual adventure. Experience taught the Church this, and she quickly associated the monastic charism of soli-tude consecrated to God with that of spiritual paternity, the purpose of which is to facilitate the full flowering of an authentic sonship in the spirit, based on baptism. There is no monk, then, without an abbot, for no one brings to birth the fullness of divine life of himself. God, the one Father, uses the mediation of experienced men, to whom He entrusts the charism of representing Him and of acting in His name, just as Christ represented the Father and acted in His name. The abbot, says Saint Benedict, holds the place of Christ, icon of the Father, and that is why he is given the name of abbot, the name the Holy Spirit places in the hearts of the children of God (cf. Rom 8: 14).

Here then is the abbot, placed at the centre of the organisation of the monastery's life, at the very heart of what is most profoundly spiritual in this life. The abbot and Christ, the abbot and the Holy Spirit, the abbot and the Father: Benedict does not hesitate to place the abbot in this divine sphere. The whole composition of the monastic edifice, in its most practical and material aspects as well as in its spiritual dimension, is thereby centred on God Himself. Christ leads the community by the abbot. As for the abbot, he serves Christ by serving his brethren. Benedict underlines the great authority that is entrusted to the abbot and consequently the great spirit of service that must animate him in all that he does. It falls to the abbot, above all, to teach. He must enlighten spirits by his word and by his example. He must help souls. To do that, he must adapt himself to each one, striving to understand his temperament and the most efficacious way to come to his aid on the path to conversion. The abbot is responsible for the obedience of his disciples, in other words for the concrete way in which they obey God. Obedience, already highlighted at the very beginning of the *Prologue* in an emphatic expression—"the very strong and glorious weapons of obedience"[6]—,occupies a central place in the spiritual edifice and in the organisation of the monastery. In one sense, it is what a Benedictine monastery guarantees to the monks. In this way, they can be sure that they are not following their own more or less vague, superficial or illusory personal intuitions or wishes. They are guided and accompanied at every step along the path of following Christ, He Himself being the Obedient One *par excellence*. They can indeed know swiftly and surely if their acts are, or are not, in line with God's will. According to Saint Paul: *"God desires all men to be saved"* (1 Tim 2: 4) and *"God's will is your sanctification"* (1 Thess 4: 3). Thus, salvation and holiness are the goal of both the abbot's authority and the disciples' obedience and what most profoundly characterises their interactions and collaboration.

In order to guide souls, the abbot must love people and give himself to all without distinction or preferences. That does not stop him from recognising virtue, manifested above all by good works, by humility and, once again, by obedience. It also falls to him to correct, tactfully, and in the manner best adapted to the capacity and temperament of the disciple. Many other passages of the *Rule* describe the abbot's role in all areas of life. Chapter 2 concentrates on his spiritual mission, the heavy responsibility entrusted to him of "governing souls and adapting himself to many dispositions".[7] There must be no question of him allowing himself to play power games or of giving too much attention to the financial or material life of the monastery. He must always remain the humble servant of Christ, the One Shepherd who has entrusted to him part of His flock and to whom he will have to render an account.

---

6   Prologue 3.
7   RB 2, 31.

Chapter 3 deals with the role all the monks must play in important decision making. Benedict does not want the abbot to be an autocrat deciding everything by himself. He obliges him to consult the brethren, and in order to do that, to assemble them and listen to them. After doing that, he will take the decision to which all must conform. But he is to provide the time and to offer them the opportunity to speak and give his full attention to what the Holy Spirit is saying to him through them, sometimes by the mouth of the youngest or humblest of the brothers. The gift of themselves, which the brothers make by their vow of obedience, requires that they be treated with respect, listened to and governed wisely and justly. Except in the case of the election of the abbot, however, Benedict does not envisage the monks having the right to vote which they have enjoyed since the modern era. The abbot calls the monks to council, not to allow them to exercise a democratic power of decision, but to share with them a process of spiritual discernment. The Holy Spirit speaks to the assembled community, everyone strives to listen to Him, the abbot ratifies the process by his final decision. Furthermore, the context is perfectly clear: "Let all follow the Rule as master of life, and let no one be rash enough to depart from it in any way whatsoever. Let no one in the monastery follow the will of his own heart".[8] No one, neither the abbot nor the monks, must turn aside from obedience to the will of God.

The first three chapters thus describe a human society completely oriented towards the work for which the monks joined the monastery. Chapters 4 to 7 will throw a decisive light on the path of conversion of heart. Chapters 8 to 20 will describe the climate of praise in which this will be accomplished. Thus the section from the *Prologue* to

---

[8]   RB 3, 7–8

chapter 20 lays down the foundations of the monastic institution.

The Path of Conversion of Heart

Chapters 4 to 7 are the heart of the *Rule*. Saint Benedict gives us here the key elements of his spiritual doctrine. Two long chapters (78 verses for Chapter 4 on the Tools of good works; 70 for Chapter 7 on Humility) stand on either side of two shorter chapters (19 verses for Chapter 5 on Obedience; 8 for Chapter 6 on Silence). The monk is invited to use the tools of good works laid down by the Gospel (Chapter 4) and to descend the ladder of humility which leads to Heaven (Chapter 7) by cultivating especially obedience (Chapter 5) and silence (Chapter 6).

Good works

Chapter 4 draws up a list of 73 good works, which are like so many "tools of the spiritual craft" to be used in the workshop which is "the enclosure of the monastery and stability in the community".[9] We find here the ten commandments as well as lists of virtues and vices drawn from the Gospel, from the letters of Saint Paul or from the homilies of the Church Fathers. Certain commandments are very general and concern the Christian life: "Not to kill, not to steal, to bury the dead, to comfort the afflicted, to utter truth from heart and mouth, to fear the day of judgement".[10] Others are applied more specifically to the monastic life and its exigencies of asceticism and charity: "To love fasting, not to love much speaking, to listen willingly to holy reading, to love chastity, to honour the

---

[9]   RB 4, 75. 78.
[10] RB 4, 3.5.17.19.28.44.

seniors, to love the young".[11] A special place is given to the precepts linked to the love of God and neighbour:

> Above all, to love God with all one's heart, with all one's soul, and with all one's strength, then one's neighbour as oneself, to prefer nothing to the love of Christ, never to forsake charity, to love one's enemies, to hate no one, not to love contention, to pray for one's enemies in the love of Christ, to make peace with one's adversaries before the sun goes down.[12]

Desiring eternal life with all spiritual longing[13] and having confidence in the mercy of God[14] show us how we are to understand a vivid awareness of the last things—death and judgement[15] —which is one of the constants of the *Rule*. In all these good works it is in fact a question of "carrying out the precepts of God each day in one's deeds".[16] Saint Benedict intends to construct in this way a solid edifice, that house, which, according to the Gospel, is built upon rock and which is likened to those who "hear my words and do them".[17] He is not building on vague mystical aspirations or on bursts of generosity with no tomorrow. He builds brick by brick, humbly laying down one act after another, with unfailing perseverance and carefully tending the flame of loving desire, which is the soul of the whole enterprise.

---

[11]   RB 4, 13.52.55.64.68.70.71.
[12]   RB 4, 1.2.21.26.31.65.71.72.
[13]   RB 4,46.
[14]   RB 4,73.
[15]   RB 4, 44.45.47.
[16]   RB 4, 63.
[17]   Prologue 33–34.

Obedience

Chapter 5 provides what looks most like a brief theology of obedience. Benedict has already assigned major importance to this. The disciple's obedience to the abbot guarantees the solidity of the whole monastic edifice, in the service of the fulfilment of God's desire to save us, revealed in Jesus Christ. Obedience thus has a threefold dimension: pedagogical for the disciple who wants to learn; prudential in bringing about wise governance of the community; and spiritual by entering into the redemptive mystery of Christ's obedience. It is this last aspect which is the most important. Obedience directs each action and one's whole life towards Christ. When the monk is obedient it is to Christ, through the person of the abbot (and of the other office-holders). At the same time, his obedience imitates that of Christ and participates in His mystery. The monk is thus obedient, both to Christ and like Christ.

With the Desert Fathers, Benedict praises prompt obedience. Has an order been given? The disciple leaves unfinished all that he was doing and accomplishes it at once. Everything happens so quickly that it is not possible to distinguish between the order and its being carried out. The superior and the monk are perfectly united in carrying out God's will. Thus it is no longer themselves acting, but God who acts in them. The perfect illustration of this prompt obedience is the miracle of Saint Maurus walking on the water, recounted in chapter 7 of the *Life* of Saint Benedict. The young monk Placid has been sent to draw water from the lake but leaning over too far, falls into the water and is carried away by the current. Benedict at once sends Maurus to look for him. Without hesitating, Maurus runs to the lake and continues running over the water of the lake, until he can seize the child and bring him back to the shore. It is only then that he realises what obedience has enabled him to do. Saint Benedict attributes the miracle to the disciple's perfect obedience, while Maurus imputes it to the abbot's holiness. The child settles the dispute: at the moment he was pulled from the water, he was aware of the presence of Benedict himself. Thus, the superior and the disciple—but more fundamentally, God and man—are united in the act of obedience. God acts through those who are obedient. He continues in them the work of salvation accomplished by the obedience of Christ. To obey, Chapter 5 tells us, is to enter into the mystery of the obedience of the Son of God as a free and loving creature.

For obedience is above all a matter of love. "It is appropriate for those who hold nothing dearer to them than Christ".[18] It comes from a heart which gives with joy.[19] One can certainly obey out of duty or fear, and these motives are not to be despised. But Christian obedience comes from the love which unites us to Christ and from the desire for eternal life,[20] towards which Christ leads us by this path of obedience. Of course, it includes a large measure of renunciation. It is impossible to carry on acting however one pleases, or following what Saint Benedict calls "self-will".[21] The obedient person, the one after Saint Benedict's own heart, "does not live according to his own personal choices, desires or passions, he walks in conformity with the judgments and orders of another, he lives in a monastery and desires to have an abbot to govern him".[22] All the strength of the cenobitic institution is once more expressed by Saint Benedict in these few words. Obedience

---

[18]   RB 5, 2.

[19]   RB 5, 16.

[20]   RB 5, 4. 10.

[21]   RB 5, 7.

[22]   RB 5, 12.

is the monastic lifestyle. By it, the monk makes his own
one of the fundamental characteristics of Christ. It makes
him like Christ. It is divinising.

Silence

The short chapter on silence adds a complementary trait
to the portrait of the disciple. In order to obey you have
to listen. In order to listen, you have to be quiet. "It is
fitting for the disciple to be silent and to listen".[23] By
keeping silence we also avoid many sins. The tongue can
do a lot of harm. In an enclosed environment it has a
surprisingly destructive force. Entering a monastery then,
means mastering silence: no discourses or chatter about
things or people, or empty words about God and the
spiritual life. Silence honours the presence and mystery of
each thing and person. Above all, it is the privileged
atmosphere for encountering God. So we will limit ourselves to such words that have some useful purpose, and
we make these as brief as possible. We will avoid vain
words. We will resolutely refrain from all evil words.[24] In
another place, Benedict says that our speech must also be
good, and that there are various degrees of silence according to the time of day, when words are often necessary,
and of night, when one can refrain from speaking almost
completely.[25]

Humility

Chapter 7 is the longest and most important of the *Rule*.
Following the Master and Cassian, Saint Benedict
describes here the monk's whole itinerary. Does he want
to go to Heaven? Let him take the Gospel path of humility:

---

[23]   RB 6, 6.
[24]   RB 6, 2.
[25]   RB 42.

"Whoever humbles himself will be exalted".[26] Ancient philosophies proposed a spiritual ascent by means of successive detachments, towards an ever higher contemplation and an ever closer union with the ineffable mystery of the divinity. The Gospel prefers the paradox of the Incarnation and the Cross. God has come down to the sinner who is lost. He has initiated the downward movement which is the only path to glory. This, then, is the path to follow. Christ has gone the whole way along it when, being divine Himself, he did not cling to His privileges, but emptied Himself, becoming a man among men, a slave among slaves, freely humbling Himself, and becoming obedient even unto death, death on the Cross. That is why God has exalted Him (cf. Phil 2: 5–11).

Benedictine humility is thus by no means the kind of modesty that refrains from overestimating our own gifts or accomplishments. By it, the monk makes the mystery of salvation his own. He harmonizes his way of being and of acting with the divine way of redemptive Incarnation. Saint Benedict, as a teacher taking care to provide eloquent images showing the stages to be followed, enriches his presentation of humility with the symbol of Jacob's ladder. In a dream the patriarch had seen angels ascending and descending on a mysterious ladder which joined heaven and earth. This ascent and descent, comments Benedict, illustrates the paradox of humility which ascends by descending. The ladder is the monk's life. The rungs are fixed in his soul and body. Humility summons his entire being and makes him enter into the mystery of divine action.

Benedict goes on then to describe the twelve degrees of this ladder. He describes a progression in one's relationship with God which passes from fear to love. Everything begins with the fear of God. For Benedict, as for the entire

---

[26] RB 7, 1, quoting Lk 14: 11 and parallels.

Bible, it is a question of a fundamental attitude. He describes fear as the echo of the awareness of the presence of God in the soul and life of the monk. Man is enfolded in the gaze of a God who fathoms him and knows him completely, who scrutinises his actions and his thoughts, from whom no desire, no movement of passion is hidden, and who is constantly being informed about His servants by His angels. It is not of course a question of tyrannical surveillance by a "Big Brother", but of loving attention taken to its divine maximum. To fear is to be seized by the mystery of God's love to the point of being pierced throughout by it. Before the God who knows me completely and whom I know so little, an awareness of excess and inequality plunges my soul into fear. Feeling the thrice holy God so near and so intimate, my whole sinful being is afraid and fears condemnation. God is living. He is supremely and continually present. He gauges all my actions. There is a hell where he casts those who resist Him and persist in evil. The monk, says St Benedict, ceaselessly thinks of all this. He places it before his eyes. He takes it very seriously and remembers it constantly, as he reminds himself that Heaven is promised to the righteous. This fear which takes hold of him also sets him free in that it causes him to hate sin and to be ever on his guard to avoid occasions of sin. It takes possession of the monk's soul in the measure that his faith and hope grow, as well as the awareness of his responsibility: a beneficent hand is held out to him, grace is offered to him, mercy always allows him a fresh start; it is up to him to respond to so much divine generosity. Benedict wants monks to be completely taken up with the reality of divine love and the urgency of responding to it.

Far from paralysing, the fear of God motivates. It strengthens freedom and enlightens the conscience. In the second degree of humility,[27] the monk understands the danger involved in following the inclinations of his own sinful heart and the arbitrariness of his own will. He gives expression to the orientation which he means to give his life in the very words of Jesus: "I have not come to do my own will, but that of him who sent me" (Jn 6: 38). The third degree sees the monk formulate a radical choice in obedience. He submits himself to a superior, a man like himself, with all his limitations, in whom he recognises God's representative, charged by Christ and the Church to show him the Father's will: "The third degree of humility is that a monk, for the love of God, submits himself to his superior in all obedience, imitating the Lord, of whom the Apostle says: 'He became obedient even unto death.'"[28] Only love, purified and set free by fear, can commit itself so resolutely to the path of obedience.

The fourth step on the ladder of humility[29] marks the entrance into the world of patience. Obedience, chosen so generously, is found to be arduous. It is not that the monk is asked to do difficult things, but rather that his relationship with his superior and his brethren turns out to be difficult and is characterised by numerous obstacles. Saint Benedict speaks of difficult and hard things, and even insults and injustices. He invites the monk to put up with a clumsy superior, to accept annoying circumstances and false brethren. Everything seems to turn against the monk who finds himself plunged in solitude and contradiction. Benedict throws an immensely positive light on this familiar human experience of an environment suddenly becoming hostile just when we were counting on it to help and sustain us. It is the time for patience: "his heart silently

---

[27] RB 7, 31–33.
[28] RB 7, 34.
[29] RB 7, 35–43.

embraces patience".[30] It is a matter of holding on and passing through the trial as a ship passes through a storm. Nevertheless, there is no question of closing in on oneself, or of becoming rigid, bitter or disillusioned. The chance is too good to be missed. Patience comes from the love which understands that the trial offers him the grace of growth. Like Jesus in His passion, the monk embraces silence and patience. He does not complain, he does not remonstrate, he does not justify himself. He suffers "for the Lord".[31] He has no doubts about the Lord's presence at his side. He has a firm hope in the recompense promised to the one who endures trial.[32] Even if he has to confront a little "death",[33] the certainty of the victory that divine grace will give him fills him with joy: "In all these things we overcome through Him who has loved us".[34] The monk receives the grace to discern the hand of God at work in a paradoxical way. Like the psalmist, he recognises that he is being tried and tested by God.[35] Far from rebelling, he grasps the invitation to even more love, love that is given to him by the very One who asks it of him. He no longer acts for himself, nor to receive the approval of others, but for God alone. As a result he enters into the evangelical freedom which allows him to respond to acts of aggression with more patience, more true generosity, wholeheartedly blessing the very people who act as his enemies. This degree of humility sets love free.

The fifth, sixth and seventh degrees bring us to humility properly so called. This begins with the recognition and

---

[30]   RB 7, 35.
[31]   RB 7, 38.
[32]   RB 7, 39.
[33]   RB 7, 38.
[34]   RB 7, 39, quoting Rom 8: 37.
[35]   RB 7, 40.

confession of sin.[36] It extends into the acceptance of
humble and humiliating circumstances.[37] It culminates in
the profound conviction that one is the least and most
insignificant of men.[38] We would be mistaken if we read
these texts as descriptions of psychological states, which
would amount to making them a defence of guiltiness and
depression. Saint Benedict does not depart from the
specifically spiritual plane. This certainly has repercus-
sions on the psychological level, but it is not to be reduced
to the play of feelings. The abundance of scriptural references (no less than eight quotations in these dozen verses)
turns the reader in the right direction. The monk does not
compare himself to anyone else. He places himself before
God. It is because he really meets Him that he comes to
recognise himself as a sinful creature, not just in some
superficial, general and as it were abstract way, but in all
the realism of his spiritual state. We could speak here of
degrees of truth. In the fifth degree, filled with an intense
hope, the monk recognises his sin and the mercy of God.
In the sixth degree, he recognises his personal poverty and
does not complain about circumstances which emphasize
it, while having a vivid awareness of always being with
God. In the seventh degree, he draws near to Christ, who,
in His Passion, took the last place, and he sings with the
psalmist: "It has been good that you humble me, so that I
might learn your commandments".[39] In bringing together
these two parts of verses from the same psalm, does not
Saint Benedict give us to understand that it is humility
which enables us to learn the commandments, that is to
say, to learn to love in the full sense of the Gospel? We

---

[36]   Fifth degree, RB 7, 44–48.
[37]   Sixth degree, RB 7, 49–50.
[38]   Seventh degree, RB 7, 51–54.
[39]   RB 7, 4, quoting Psalm 118: 71, 73.

probably reach here the heart of the paradox of Benedictine humility. It has no meaning, it is even dangerous, if it
is not an impulse thoroughly imbued with charity. Humility is the fire of love taking hold of the soul in fear,
purifying it in obedience, patience and humiliation, in
order to lead it to the fullness of the gift.

Before reaching this final stage, Saint Benedict conse-
crates the following degrees to the more outward consequences of the work of humility. We might speak of
degrees of effacement. In the eighth degree,[40] the monk
merges into the life of the community whose *Rule* and
example he follows. He no longer has any need or desire
to be different. The ninth,[41] tenth[42] and eleventh degrees[43]
show a silent monk, master of his tongue and of his
laughter, capable of saying the right and appropriate words
at the suitable time. Far from being inhibited, he shines in
St. Benedict's eyes as a wise and well balanced person.
Humility makes us human, deflates the swollen ego and
shows in its full light the unique dignity of the person.

Thus it is a mature, flourishing man who comes to the
twelfth degree of humility and reaches the top of the
ladder.[44] Wherever he is, whatever he is doing, his life is
one. Humility radiates even from his physical posture. It
has become the natural inclination of his being. There he
stands, in the truth, not before the eyes of men, but under
the gaze of God whose holiness condemns him and whose
mercy lifts him up again. He has attained an evangelical
summit, since Saint Benedict compares him to the tax
collector who humbly confesses his sin and whom God

---

[40]   RB 7, 55.
[41]   RB 7, 56–58.
[42]   RB 7, 59.
[43]   RB 7, 60–61.
[44]   RB 7, 62–66.

justifies (cf. Lk. 18). He remains permanently under the formidable, fascinating and overwhelming gaze of the God of love. He abides in this lowest place towards which the Most High bends down with predilection. He knows that he is loved even in his lack of love. He remains overwhelmed by so much love and mercy. Tears of contrition and thanksgiving spring from his silent heart.

At the summit of the ladder,[45] he enters into complete freedom to love. He reaches "that love of God, which, being perfect, casts out fear".[46] He does everything with ease and joy. He is constantly moved by the love of Christ. He has been purified by the Lord, and the Holy Spirit has accomplished His work in him.

Such is the monk after Saint Benedict's heart. The hidden pride of his soul has been broken by divine love. Humbly and simply he takes his place as a creature caught up in the movement of love which comes forth from the Father and bends down over the world in Jesus Christ in order to reconcile him to God through the sacrifice of the Cross and bring him to the fullness of his filial dignity by the gift of the Holy Spirit. From the depths of his poverty, visited by infinite love, he gives thanks and glory to the Trinitarian God. His heart resounds with a constant doxology which finds its ecclesial expression in the liturgical life of the monastery which chapters eight to twenty are going to present. He has become praise and universal intercession.

Chapter 7 of the *Rule*, whose paradoxical character could be confusing, is offered as the mature fruit of the wisdom of monastic life from its origins in Egypt at the time of Saint Antony the Great (251–356). It sums up the experience and teaching of generations of holy monks. It

---

[45]   RB 7, 67–70.
[46]   RB 7, 67.

is also appropriate to read it in the context of the theology
of the Fathers of the Church, in particular their vision of
the place of man in the divine plan and their theology of
grace. Chapter 7 clearly marks out the way of return to the
Father following Christ, of which the *Prologue* speaks
(Prologue 2–3). It does not give a method to follow or
exercises to do. It makes us enter into a spirit, that which
is at work in the plan of love of our God who, by saving us
humbly, teaches us humility and makes a gift of it to us.

The Work of God

The fourth and last stage of the foundation of the monastic
edifice—after the invitation of the *Prologue*, putting in
place the structures of cenobitism in the first three chapters, and teaching the fundamental attitudes of a monk's
life in Chapters 4 to 7—consists in organising the service
of praise, which is the community's first and principal
activity. Just as the liturgy would be exterior, empty
worship, if it were not accompanied by the work of
conversion, moral effort would likewise be doomed to
failure if it did not constantly return to prayer and the
Eucharist as its source and summit.

When speaking of the liturgy, Saint Benedict uses the
Latin expression *Opus Dei*, which is translated as "the
Work of God". We are to understand that this concerns a
work which is not only done *for* God, but which concerns
God directly, which has God as its *object*. Praise can even
be said to be a divine work, and divinising, for it originates
in the gift of God, the superabundance of which it celebrates. It is carried out by the Church in union with Christ,
who is both High Priest and cantor of the eternal praise.
The work of the liturgy, which is the source, summit and
end of the Church's works, naturally occupies the central

place in the monk's activities and timetable. Seven times a day and once at night, the community assembles in the oratory of the monastery. Its praise is based principally on the biblical psalter, with its one hundred and fifty psalms, which Benedict envisages being recited each week.

The Night Office, celebrated towards the end of the night, before daybreak, has the character of a long vigil. The singing of twelve psalms, in two groups of six, is preceded by two introductory psalms repeated every day, and punctuated by readings drawn from Holy Scripture and the Fathers of the Church. On Sundays and feast days, a series of three biblical canticles is added. This precedes a final patristic reading and the solemn singing of the Sunday or feast day gospel.

The daytime is divided up between the two major offices—Lauds in the morning and Vespers in the evening—and four shorter offices which mark the hours of the ancient day: Prime at the first hour (7 am), Terce at the third hour (9 am), Sext at the sixth hour (noon) and None at the ninth hour (3 pm). The office of Compline, at the end of the day, uses the same psalms each day. It precedes the great silence of the night. Saint Benedict takes the variations in light from one season to another into account, subtlely modifying the timetable. Thus the Night Office is reduced in summer when the nights are shorter. The liturgical seasons also dictate various adjustments, especially in Lent and Eastertide.

Saint Benedict carefully arranges the psalms over these various hours. He lays down many ceremonial details. He foresees cases in which the abbot may or must introduce slight modifications. He clearly defines the most important parts and those which can, if necessary, be omitted. He indicates how much singing there should be, in proportion to the number and strength of the community. As in his entire *Rule*, he shows himself both precise in his prescriptions and broad-minded when it comes to adapting to particular circumstances. Above all, he is intent on fixing a measure that is neither too ambitious nor too lax, so that the Work of God may be carried out worthily.

Two short chapters close this section, one on how to sing the psalms,[47] the other on prayer.[48] They are of capital importance for those who consecrate such a large part of their life to communal and personal prayer. Nevertheless they are remarkably concise. The chapter on communal prayer is meant to help the monk find the right interior disposition. For this, the fundamental element is taking into account the presence of God. God is present everywhere, as the first degree of humility insistently reminded us, but at the Office, where we address ourselves explicitly to Him, our awareness of His presence must be even more lively. Thus the liturgical celebration unfolds in a climate of fear. There is no question of becoming accustomed to God's nearness: Benedict wants his monks to be imbued with a sense of mystery. To God who is present the monk responds with his own presence, and in particular, by his attention to the text he is singing. Benedict invites us to have our mind and voice in harmony, to bring about a concord between the text being sung and the heart of the singer. When the exterior act thus accords with the interior act, it is the Word which assures their unity. This instruction must first be understood as an invitation to attention and even concentration. The monk, penetrated by his sense of the presence of God, strives to engage his whole being with the act of praise. He pronounces the words as well as possible, and his mind and his heart are in complete rapport with what he is singing. This is the

---

[47]   RB 19.
[48]   RB 20.

one and only piece of advice the *Rule* gives about the exercise of choral prayer. It says a great deal about Saint Benedict's confidence in the psalms. To sing the psalms is to surrender to them, to give them our voice and our mind, with the assurance that these inspired texts offer our souls the right attitudes in our relationship with God. The Psalter provides us with material for our choral prayer, but even more, it constitutes a rule for it. Following in the footsteps of the great patristic commentators, Saint Athanasius and Saint Augustine, Saint Benedict takes it for granted that all prayer is contained in the psalms, and that the psalms are therefore the school of prayer *par excellence*. For Benedict, whoever sings the psalms in the office, in the atmosphere of reverential fear which goes with faith in the divine presence, learns just by doing this how to address God, how to ask Him for His graces and to thank Him, how to praise Him and adore Him.

Chapter 20 on private prayer comes from the same approach to the mystery of prayer. The atmosphere for this more personal time which the monk is invited to give is one of humility and purity of devotion. Thus let him use few words, and present rather a pure heart and tears of compunction.[49] In prayer, it is not the man that matters, nor his various levels of feeling or understanding, but God, to whose presence the one praying exposes himself entirely as to a consuming fire of love, justice and mercy. The confession of past faults, accompanied by tears of repentance, will thus often be included in this prayer.[50] But Benedict does not rule out the possibility that the Holy Spirit may prompt a prolongation of the encounter, and that He may become the master of prayer, drawing the soul into the depths of God. Once again, it is not so much

---

[49]   RB 20, 2–3.
[50]   cf. RB 4, 57 & 49, 4.

the Christian praying as the Spirit of God praying in his heart that is important.

Praying to God with God's words and God's Spirit: such is prayer as Saint Benedict sees it. This kind of prayer, entirely centred on the mystery of the Trinity at work in the life of the Church, may readily be likened to the prayer of the tax collector referred to in the twelfth degree of humility. The sinner humbly prostrates himself confessing his sins. The Spirit lifts him up to bring him into the pure joy of God. Tears accompany the entire journey which goes from repentance to praise and which transforms the monk into a universal intercessor.

The Four Pillars

In the Rule's teaching up to Chapter 20, Saint Benedict describes the foundations of the monastic edifice. The *Prologue* evokes the relationship of love which leads the monk towards God in response to His paternal call. Chapters 1 to 3 make the relationship between the abbot and the monks within the monastery the basis of cenobitism. Chapters 4 to 7 describe the spiritual path of conversion. Finally, chapters 8 to 20 introduce us into the climate of continual prayer characteristic of the monastery. We could represent these stages under the symbol of four pillars:

- The first pillar describes the *mystery*: Benedictine monasticism is an adventure of love initiated by the Trinitarian love manifested in Jesus Christ.
- The second pillar defines *place*: the monastery and the community structured by the relationship of obedience to the abbot. This is the pillar of Benedictine cenobitism.

- The third pillar is that of the *path*: the spiritual art which consists of descending in humility in order to open oneself up to love.

- The fourth pillar foresees the rhythms of *time* and organises the continual dialogue of the soul with God which is the prayer of praise drawn from the Psalter.

In Chapter 58, which deals with the reception of new brothers, Benedict picks up these same elements again. The Novice Master must ascertain above all whether the newcomer "truly seeks God".[51] This is the first pillar. Whoever is not ready for the heart's adventure with God has nothing to do with the monastery. Next he must see whether the candidate is zealous for the Work of God (the fourth pillar), obedience (the second pillar), and humiliations (the third pillar). Knowledge of the Psalter[52] and of the *Rule*[53] occupy a special place in formation, which also includes clear warnings about "the hard and difficult things by which we go to God" and a serious examination of the candidate's patience.[54]

To ensure that the adventure of love in the footsteps of Christ does not flounder in the sand Saint Benedict thus sets up a school of the Lord's service. He lays the monastery on the firm foundations of the obedience of all to the Rule and the Abbot. The monk who perseveres there learns the spiritual art of conversion, which progressively renders him more free for communion of love with God and with neighbour. Receiving all from God, from whom he asks for all in continual prayer, he becomes a cantor of that praise which, in the Church, constantly renders glory to the Trinity of love. The monastery is the place where the

---

[51]   RB 58, 7.

[52]   RB 8, 3; fourth pillar.

[53]   RB 58, 9.12.13; second pillar.

[54]   RB 58, 8.11; third pillar.

baptised person, surrendering himself without reserve to the love of Christ, is guided along a tried and tested path of conversion and is led to open himself to a grace of communion and praise, in the heart of the mystery of the Church.

Works and Days

Saint Benedict does not limit himself to an exposition of principles, however luminous. More than fifty further chapters describe the way in which the pillars of the monastic ideal support the daily life of a human group in all its aspects. The author of the *Rule* reviews the actions of the monk's life and gives practical indications about how to use these pillars within the monastic framework. Whether it is a matter of eating or sleeping, of clothing or ownership, of reading or work, of making, buying or selling, of welcoming, of receiving a new candidate or sending someone away, of making mistakes or being corrected, and so on, the *Rule* covers each concrete situation. It formulates general principles, while often leaving the superior and the monk room to manoeuvre in order to adapt to particular circumstances of place and time. With its flair for shedding light on the details of his existence by focusing on the goal the monk has in view, the *Rule* establishes a unified and highly coherent form of life.

Saint Benedict's wisdom lies especially in the equilibrium and proportion which characterise his approach. He knows how to show himself exacting with regard to the essential, while being flexible and moderate regarding secondary things. He himself practices perfectly the advice he gives to the abbot:

> Let him be prudent and considerate in his commands whether the work which he enjoins concern God or the world, let him be discreet and moderate

in all things, remembering the discretion of holy
Jacob, who said: 'If I cause my flocks to be over-
driven they will all perish in a day.' (Gen 33, 13) So,
imitating these and other examples of discretion,
which is the mother of virtues, let him so temper
all things that the strong may still have something
to long after, and the weak may not draw back.[55]

As we can see, Saint Benedict's moderation—the "discretion" Saint Gregory already spoke of so highly—has
nothing to do with a lack of generosity. It springs from a
recognition of the fact that not everyone has the same
strength or ability. Benedict pays careful attention to the
weakest. His intention is to help them by the authority of
the *Rule*, and he wants the abbot and the brethren to do
the same. Far from legislating for pure spirits, Benedict
shows that he is profoundly human. We can judge that the
care he took to provide for the reality of human nature
contributed enormously to the spread of his *Rule*. He knew
how to draw practical consequences from the fact that
God's call is addressed to men who have limited abilities
and who are marked by sin. He abounds in mercy and
affectionate compassion towards all, and teaches others
to do likewise.

The last chapters of the *Rule*,[56] which people have
sometimes thought were added in a second redaction, give
even greater attention to the quality of fraternal relationships. For Benedict, it is not a matter of fostering these to
the detriment of the obedient relationship of each monk
with the abbot, or of the above all supernatural bond which
unites them with each other. Thus Chapter 68 provides
for a respectful dialogue between the monk who has
received a difficult or impossible command, and the abbot.

[55]   RB 64, 17–19.
[56]   RB 67–72.

Once again, the abbot has the last word, and obedience to
his final decision is required, but, says Saint Benedict, this
obedience must proceed from charity. Likewise, it is in all
charity and solicitude that the monks are invited to obey
one another.[57] There can be no question of one brother
correcting another without an explicit authorisation from
the abbot,[58] or of defending a brother who has been
corrected by the abbot, even if he is a relative.[59] Thus,
fraternal charity is not to be confused with any kind of
affective affinity between certain brethren which would
compromise in one way or another the seriousness of their
obedience. On the other hand, authentic charity is shown
precisely by what allows a more perfectly generous obedience.

   Chapter 72 on "good zeal" offers a concise synthesis of
Saint Benedict's ideal. In it, he paints a portrait of the
monk for whom charity, the good zeal of love, is the
guiding principle of his whole life and of his dealings with
his brothers, with the abbot and with God. Love of the
brethren begins with giving them honour: paying attention
to their dignity as children of God, created for His glory
and redeemed by the Blood of Christ.[60] It is then expressed
in limitless patience with their weaknesses, whatever they
may be.[61] It goes on to blossom into an ever more perfect
mutual obedience and emulation in the pursuit of virtue.[62]
Forgetfulness of self, encouraging us to give first place to
others, is one of its important manifestations .[63] A chaste
affection, which does not strive to attract or possess,

---

[57]   RB 71.
[58]   RB 70.
[59]   RB 69.
[60]   RB 72, 4.
[61]   RB 72, 5.
[62]   RB 72, 6.
[63]   RB 72, 7.

renders this purified fraternal charity truly human.[64] Similarly, love sets the tone in the monk's relationship with God. It inspires the reverent fear he has for Him which remains a proper characteristic of supernatural charity.[65] Affection for the abbot, far from blunting the authority which obedience recognises that he has, is accompanied by an equally deep humility which takes nothing away from its sincerity.[66] Finally, Christ stands at the centre of loving relations as the One who, loved above all, liberates true love, ever more intense, for each brother, for the abbot and for God.[67] It is in Him that the communion of love, which is the soul of the community, is bound together. He recognises in it His body, composed of members who grow together, and whom He, as a Good Shepherd, guides towards eternal life.[68]

In the last chapter, Saint Benedict sums up his intention and recalls what his purpose has been. He has written his *Rule* for beginners. He wants to help them to make a good start. As an experienced teacher filled with wisdom, he sets out to render them the most useful and the most difficult service: that of teaching them the basic principles of the spiritual craft and of furnishing them with an appropriate setting in which to exercise it. He humbly refers to the masters who have preceded him. The disciples themselves can draw with profit from their writings in due time. But let them begin at the beginning, and with Christ's help put his instructions into practice. God will lead them further and higher when He judges it opportune. When sanctity is the goal of our lives, it is good to begin humbly

---

[64] RB 72, 8.
[65] RB 72, 9.
[66] RB 72, 10.
[67] RB 72, 11.
[68] RB 72, 12.

and to learn to leave it to God Himself to lead us into the fullness of His mystery of love.

2 FRAGMENTS FROM A HISTORY OF THE BENEDICTINE FAMILY

I T WAS PRINCIPALLY through the *Rule* of St. Benedict that monasticism spread in the West and in countries influenced by the West's missionary expansion. The *Rule* was linked to the very existence of monasticism as a permanent dimension of the Church's life. Wherever evangelisation has been sufficiently profound, the monastic call to consecrate oneself totally to Christ within a community dedicated to the praise of God always resonates in Christian hearts. However urgent the need to proclaim the Gospel or minister to souls may be, monasticism bears witness to the longing always to give first place to the worship of God. The Church's apostolic activity is carried out on the basis of the unceasing prayer of monks and nuns. Without this contemplative foundation, all the Church's activity would soon lose its significance.

The *Rule*'s flexibility and openness have made it possible for Saint Benedict's spirit to be lived out in many and various ways across the centuries. Each monastery—and in a sense, each monk, each nun—writes an original page in the history of the Benedictine family. Rather than giving a detailed description of the whole picture, the following pages aim to try to suggest Saint Benedict's spiritual fecundity in the course of the centuries by focusing on some fragments. Each time, a biographical or historical sketch will be followed by a short spiritual text. May the reader feel invited to explore the immense riches of the Saint Benedict's heritage!

Bede the Venerable or Love for the Word

One can only be struck by the long hours that Saint Benedict assigns to the reading of the Word of God. He calls this activity *lectio divina*. It is a reading of the word of God, transmitted in the Bible and commented on by the Fathers of the Church: a reading which puts us in contact with God, a reading attentive to the voice of God. After the Divine Office, it occupies an amount of time comparable to that for work. The monastic life is for those who are in love with the Word.

It found one such of exceptional fervour in the person of Saint Bede the Venerable (672–735). Probably of a modest origin, Bede was entrusted at the age of seven to the monastery of Saints Peter and Paul at Wearmouth. This had recently been founded by Saint Benedict Biscop in Northumbria in the north of England. Returning from a journey to Rome, this English Benedict brought the *Rule* of Saint Benedict. On this base, he founded Wearmouth in 674 and Jarrow in 682, two monasteries destined to unprecedented expansion (by 716 there were about six hundred monks between these two houses). In 680 he also invited the Roman precantor John to come and teach the community the Roman chant. For these communities on the frontiers of Christianity, the atmosphere was one of romanisation and internationalisation.

The young Bede is thus formed in the regular life with its alternation of offices, reading and work. He has a perfect mastery of Latin and classical culture, and some idea of Greek and Hebrew. All his life, he studies Holy Scripture, writing commentaries on it and teaching it to the young monks. He also becomes a specialist in history. He remains to this day the principal source for our knowledge of the history of the English peoples and of their evangelisation. A deacon at nineteen, a priest at thirty, he rarely leaves his monastery. On the other hand, he keeps up a vast monastic and literary correspondence with friends all over England and as far away as Rome.

His perspective in his approach to the word of God is not one of erudition. He wants to ensure access to an authentic text and to authorised commentaries. He has a strong vision of the teaching Church, centred on the magisterial responsibility of Peter and his successors, underlining the importance of this in the face of Celtic particularities that have held sway in the north of the British Isles for centuries. The monk reads the Bible as a member of the Church. He receives it within the community of believers. He meditates on it within the interpretive tradition handed on by the Fathers. *Lectio divina* only puts him into contact with God in so far as he is part of the community of faith to whom the Word is addressed, and whom the Spirit endows with a charism of truth when transmitting and interpreting it.

Saint Bede is still much loved by monks and nuns who recognise in him a beautiful ideal of love for the regular life, of fidelity to the Word, of humble charity and of a sense of the true Church: all characteristics of the Benedictine spirit as it has been handed down through the centuries. The importance of his historical and biblical works were decisive for medieval England. It is one of the first examples of the contribution to the cultural life and to the formation of the civilisation that we habitually connect with the name of Saint Benedict.

> Let us purify by faith the powerful vessels of our
> hearts, with the purifying force of heavenly pre-

cepts. Let us fill them with the water of knowledge of salvation, redoubling our attention to sacred readings. Let us pray to the Lord that he may make the grace of understanding, which He gives, burn with His love, for fear that it may puff us up with vainglory. May He also turn our souls towards the constant search for the things that are above to the point that we savour them so much that we are drunk with them and can sing with the Prophet: 'You have made us drink the wine of compunction.' Thus to the extent that we make progress we will be able to know in part even now the glory that Jesus will reveal perfectly in the world to come and in which He lives and reigns with the Father in the unity of the Holy Spirit for ever and ever. Amen.[1]

Cluny or The Glory of the Liturgy

As William of Aquitaine founds the Abbey of Cluny in 910, he cannot imagine the great growth and influence this new monastery will know. Very soon the house will be directly under the Holy See, all its possessions considered as entrusted to the holy Apostles Peter and Paul. It is a matter of getting round the interference of local lords, who have done so much harm to abbeys, and of allowing the restoration of what is now called the *ordo monasticus*. When Saint Odo succeeds the first abbot, Berno, in 927, he thus insists on fidelity to the *Rule* of Saint Benedict and to the customs introduced by Saint Benedict of Aniane (747–821), the great reformer of monastic life in the era of Charlemagne. With monasteries being founded in towns, and monks being ordained priests, monastic life begins to look rather different. The influence of a more developed basilical liturgy, and the more important role

---

[1]   Saint Bede, *Homily on the Gospel of the Marriage Feast at Cana.*

accorded to study, as well as the copying of manuscripts, become characteristic of Benedictine life.

Cluny gives first place to liturgical prayer, which sees there an unprecedented development. Devotion to Our Lady and the Saints, as well as prayers for the dead, come to hold an important place. Besides the Benedictine Office, a little Office of Our Lady and an Office of the Dead are integrated into the daily liturgy. Two Masses are celebrated each day. The length and splendour of the liturgies emphasizes the glory of the Most High God. The monastery is seen as a house of prayer where the monks intercede constantly for the living and the dead, particularly for its founders and benefactors. Monasticism is now resplendent and very prestigious, because it makes possible the quest for a pure life, because of its service of intercession and because of its openness to the transcendent which it secures for all of society.

Cluny rapidly becomes the head of a large number of more or less important houses in France and throughout Europe. Besides hundreds of small priories or abbeys which depend directly on the Abbey of Cluny, other monasteries are influenced by the Burgundian monastery, adopt its customs or are in constant relations with it. Cluny's example also radiates in abbeys as important as those of Aurillac, Jumièges and Fleury in France, or Saint-Paul-outside-the-walls and Subiaco in Italy. Under Saint Odilo it is then Spain with which links will intensify.

A series of great abbots, all saints, gives the abbey considerable prestige. In the period from about 950 to 1150, Odo, Mayeul, Odilo, Hugh and Peter the Venerable construct the largest church in Christendom, preside at sumptuous liturgies, found, federate or reform hundreds of monastic houses, have political and financial dealings with kings, emperors and popes, offer hospitality to multitudes of pilgrims and feed a huge number of the poor. Architecture, sculpture, manuscript illumination, the art of painting frescos and of making vestments and liturgical objects flourish, for nothing is too beautiful for God. The worship offered Him lights up the whole of society: it guarantees peace, creates a taste for order and beauty and calms anguish about death and salvation.

Under these eminent superiors we find a whole army of monks and nuns dedicated body and soul to the service of God, principally in liturgical prayer. Cluny is a house of silence and adoration. It is a community of charity and culture. The establishment of the "Truce of God", fostered by the Cluniacs, puts a limit to feudal wars and contributes to the peace and prosperity of society.

> Given that, according the words of Our Lord, everything in the Law and the Prophets is subject to the law of charity, who would pretend that the *Rule* of Saint Benedict does not fall under the same law of love? Is it possible for this *Rule*, which was established by the Holy Spirit, not to be subject to the law of Love? The *Rule* must therefore always consider charity as its mistress and allow itself to be governed by decrees of love. If the object of the *Rule* is not charity, then the *Rule* no longer has meaning. We have not made profession to follow the *Rule* without love. We do not put it into practice without loving. Thus, when we practice the commandment of love, we also keep the *Rule* and we fulfil our duty towards God.[2]

---

[2]   Peter the Venerable, *Letter* to Saint Bernard.

Cîteaux or The Grace of the Desert

The immense success of Cluny, however, does not allow us to identify purely and simply Benedictine monasticism with it. Indeed, the Cluniac experiment is controversial. In 1098, Robert, Alberic and Stephen, monks of the Benedictine Abbey of Molesmes, arrive in the solitude of Cîteaux, where they found a "new monastery". They place themselves distinctly in reaction against the liturgical and architectural inflation of the Cluniac model. They want to return to the *Rule*, observed in its simplicity and fullness, without later additions which have transformed the life of the monks to the point of rendering it almost unrecognisable. It is a matter of returning to the desert, the cradle of monasticism, and to all its fundamental values: separation from the world, solitude, poverty, simplicity, obedience, austerity, which are so many pledges of a truly evangelical joy. A simpler liturgy, serious manual labour which ensures a certain freedom in relation to lay benefactors, the absence of schools, the institution of lay brothers, dedicated to manual labour, become the marks of this new monastic style.

The arrival of Bernard and his thirty companions in 1113 will transform this rather modest endeavour into a source of monastic renewal. Bernard, who is sent as early as 1115 to found the monastery of Clairvaux, brings with him his extensive education and refined literary formation, his oratorical skills and the powerful charm of an exceptional personality. He fascinates with his eloquence, he enlightens with his teaching, he inflames with his love. With him, monastic life's centre of gravity shifts imperceptibly from the communal celebration of the liturgy and the objectivity of public worship towards the more private sphere of intimate encounter with God and its reverberations in the life of the soul. He who is called the last of the

Church Fathers, so thoroughly has he made their teaching his own, is also one of the first to formulate the laws of the interior life, to examine its movements closely and to suggest its mystery.

In his wake, the Cistercian Order experiences an extraordinary expansion. Bernard himself makes sixty-eight foundations, and Cîteaux comprises seven hundred monks at his death in 1153. The Order then brings together three hundred and thirty-nine monasteries. Three centuries later it will number almost seven hundred. Considerable demographic growth, the appeal of a simple, well-organised life-style and the strength of a centralised order, in which identical customs can be handed on, partly explain this enormous success. This is accompanied by abundant literature—that of the Cistercian Fathers. By being rooted in scripture, liturgy and patristics, it depends on traditional monastic theology and represents a form of resistance to the nascent, more intellectual, theology of the universities. It insists particularly on the loving encounter between God and man, not only in the mystery of the Church, but even in each individual soul, in the rhythm of its prayer and charity. In its own right, Cistercian spirituality constitutes an entire chapter in the history of spirituality; it deserves a much more developed presentation than the few lines we sketch here.

Cîteaux represents a sort of second wave in the monastic impetus that seizes western Europe between 1000 and 1300. Like Cluny, its star will end up by growing pale towards the end of the Middle Ages. Society and the Church will then turn towards new forms of religious life, more adapted to the life which was beginning to be concentrated in towns. The spread of the *commendum*—giving the abbatial title to persons outside the community with a share in the monastery's revenues and a consequent weakening of the monastic institution itself—is very harmful to the great orders in this period. Alongside faithful houses, but with considerably reduced strength, others fall into decadence and will only rise again through the reforms which, from 16th century will begin to be implemented in numerous monasteries through the momentum of the Council of Trent.

> *"I am the flower of the fields and the lily of the valleys."* While the Bride draws attention to the bed, the Bridegroom, on the contrary, shows her the field and prompts her to work, and he has no better inducement to propose for her than Himself as the exemplar and reward. *"I am the flower of the fields."* These words give us to understand that He is the model of either the soldier or the glory of the victor. You are both to me, O Jesus: my model in my suffering and the reward for my patience. By the example of your courage, you train my hands for war, and after victory you crown me with your majesty. Whether I see you fighting, or whether I look to you not only to crown me but to be yourself my very crown, You attract me wonderfully to yourself, and these two considerations are a powerful chain to draw me on. *"Draw me after you"* then; with what joy will I follow you! But how much sweeter it is to enjoy you! If you are so good, O Lord, for those who follow you, what will you be to those who join you? *"I am the flower of the field;"* let him who loves me come into the field, let him not refuse to fight with me, that he may be able to say: *"I have fought the good fight."*[3]

---

[3]   St Bernard, *Sermon 47 on the Song of Songs*.

Gertrude of Helfta or The Freedom to Love

In 1229, a new Benedictine monastery is founded in
Saxony. The community, which soon aligns itself with the
Cistercian Order (without, it seems, ever being completely
integrated into it, at least in the beginning), is transferred
to Helfta towards 1260 during the abbacy of Gertrude of
Hackeborn (abbess from 1251 to 1291). The abbey very
quickly distinguishes itself by its high level of culture. The
classical disciplines of grammar and the liberal arts are
taught there, and theological studies and chant are fostered. The influence of Saint Bernard and of his spousal
spirituality, which admirably unites the Bible, the liturgy
and mysticism, is very fruitful. Three exceptional individuals give the community a very particular brilliance. First
of all Mechtilde of Hackeborn (1241–1298), a first rate
musician to whom is attributed *The Book of Special Grace*.
Another Mechtilde, called Mechtilde of Magdeburg
(1207–1282), is a Béguine who ends her days in the
convent, bringing there her taste for visions and mysticism, in a style both prophetic and apocalyptic. Finally,
there is Gertrude called the Great (1256–1301). She is
entrusted as a child to the monastery where she flourishes
in a most exceptional way. With a gift for letters and the
arts, she experiences, from her "conversion" in Advent
1280 onwards, an intense mystical and literary life. Besides
the *Herald of Divine Love* (of which only the second book,
which is autobiographical, seems to be actually written by
her) and the *Exercises* (written entirely by her), she very
probably participates in the redaction of Saint Mechtilde's
Book of Special Grace.

Very Benedictine, Gertrude draws her life from the *Rule*
and the Liturgy. Although learned, she seeks the simplicity
of a prayer springing from a heart purified by the Holy
Spirit by means of monastic asceticism. Very Cistercian

in inspiration, she lives the Liturgy, and its overflowing in the dialogue of the soul with God as a mystical encounter with Christ, Spouse of the soul and of the Church. It is during an antiphon or a Psalm verse for a liturgical feast or when she is carrying out a particular function in the liturgy that the Lord manifests Himself to her. In particular, He attracts her to His Heart, opening it up to her and inviting her to dwell in it. In return, Gertrude receives Jesus into her own heart. The Bridegroom and the bride exchange their hearts in a reciprocal gift of love overflowing with life, light and joy. Gertrude is drawn to a praise that is ever more full of admiration and gratitude for Christ's love. The Cistercian attention to the humanity of Jesus gives Gertrude's Eucharistic life a very intimate and personal dimension of encounter with Christ. She longs to see with the Heart of Christ, to know Christ, to know herself and all things in Christ.

She formulates all this in simple, elegant and musical language, in which Scriptural and liturgical references are everywhere. For her, spiritual life is the full unfolding of baptism and of monastic consecration, through making her own in a very personal way the spousal dialogue of Christ and the Church in the liturgy. She achieves a kind of synthesis between the thoroughly ecclesial liturgical mysticism of Cluny and the personal relationship with the humanity of Christ inherited from Cîteaux and from Saint Bernard. She probably presents us with one of the most harmonious and complete expressions of the spiritual life that the *Rule* of Saint Benedict makes possible: an ardent path of love in the footsteps of Christ, wherein the soul yields herself to her Beloved in a way that is intimate and profoundly free, and He, in return, places her at the heart of the Church to adore, praise and intercede.

O love! Finding joy in You is the most merciful
bond between the divine Word and the soul, it is
perfect union with God. To enjoy this relationship
with you is to be mingled with your essence;
finding joy in you is becoming one single thing with
God. You are the peace which surpasses all feelings,
the sure path which leads the Bride to the nuptial
chamber. O you, who are the source of eternal
light, draw me to you in the immense depth of your
divine essence whence came forth the act which
created me. There I shall know as I am known, I
shall love as I am loved; I shall see you, O my God,
as you are, with a vision and possession which will
be my beatitude for ever.[4]

Dame Gertrude More or The Gift of Contemplation

Is it enough to be Saint Thomas More's great-great-grand-
daughter to have a monastic vocation? Helen More (1607–
1633) does not think so when against her will she joins
several cousins and a handful of young women from
English Catholic families at the abbey of Cambrai, in 1623.
She receives the habit on the last day of the year and makes
profession on 1st January 1625, thus becoming Dame
Gertrude, according to the appellation in use among the
English Benedictines. Outwardly, she conforms to what
seems to be her destiny as the daughter of a numerous
family. But her extrovert and worldly temperament is
ill-suited to the conventual life. Reading pious works, often
changing confessor, asking advice here, there and everywhere does not help. She is wasting away rather than living
when she resolves to consult a new confessor whom she
had initially mocked. To these nuns, who had been taught
a form of meditation using the imagination inspired by

---

[4]   St Gertrude, *Exercise to Stir up in Oneself The Love of God.*

the Jesuit tradition, the English Benedictine Dom Augustine Baker (1575–1641) brings something quite different: a love for the *Rule*, reference to the desert Fathers and monastic tradition, teaching about the contemplative life as set forth by classical authors, especially Julian of Norwich (*Revelations*), Walter Hilton (*The Scale of Perfection*) and the anonymous author of *The Cloud of Unknowing*, as well as the spiritual masters of Rhineland tradition, Tauler and Suso. In a short time, Gertrude's life is transformed. She loves to say that the holy monk has made what seemed impossible to her "simple and easy". She thus learns to set aside her self-will, to listen to the voice of God and to recognise the call or the inspirations of the Holy Spirit in her heart. Her fear and her despair disappear. Henceforth she can yield herself entirely to divine Love.

Gertrude's life will not be long. When Dom Augustine Baker is accused of introducing new, indeed heretical, doctrines, she is one of those who write a defence of his spiritual teaching. The father is completely exonerated, but very soon afterwards, a smallpox epidemic carries off Dame Gertrude at the age of twenty seven, on the 17th August 1633. Dom Augustine Baker prepares her spiritual writings for publication in 1658 under the title of *The Spiritual Exercises of Dame Gertrude More*, adding a biography.

Dame Gertrude More is representative of the numerous fervent nuns who fill the cloisters in the post-Reformation centuries. Often coming from aristocratic families, they preside over the destinies of numerous communities where they introduce reform, a return to the *Rule* of Saint Benedict, and a passion for the loving encounter with God.

> Shall not my soul be subject to God? O my Lord,
> far be it from me to will or desire anything but
> according to Thy will, which alone is holy. Let me
> never resist Thy will, signified to me by any means

whatsoever. Let my soul be wholly turned into a flame of Divine love, that I may aspire and attend to nothing else but Thyself alone. Blot out my sins, that my soul may return to Thee by love, from Whom by sin it has strayed. Oh ! let nothing but this desire of Thee, my God, possess my heart. Let that be my solace in labours, pains, temptations, desolations, and all afflictions of body or mind. Let not my heart, drawn by Thee to seek after nothing but love, be so base as to covet, desire, and rest in anything but Thee. Thou art my Life, my Choice, and my only Beloved. When I hear Thee but named, my Lord God, it forcibly draweth me into myself, that I may attend unto Thee, forgetting myself and whatsoever else besides Thee. For which benefit be Thou infinitely praised. Amen.[5]

Dom Guéranger or The Church at Prayer

Since the beginning of the modern era, the suppression of monasteries has become a recurrent phenomenon in the political and religious history of several countries: the dissolution in Henry VIII's England, secularisation in the Habsburg empire, suppression by the French Revolution, closure following on from the Napoleonic conquests in Europe, the *Kulturkampf* of the second half of the 19th Century in Germany and in Switzerland, the laws about association at the beginning of the 20th Century in France. Nevertheless, everywhere monastic life according to the *Rule* has started up again. It has even blossomed again in the Protestant churches, despite their inherited criticism of the religious life.

France at the beginning of the 19th Century no longer knows what a monk is. All the Benedictine monasteries

---

[5]   Dame Gertrude More, *Forty Eighth Confession of Love.*

have been suppressed. A small number of houses of Benedictine nuns have survived the trial in a semi-clandestine way and have succeeded in reassembling. The abbeys of the reformed Cistercian tradition, also called "Trappists", from the name of the Abbey of La Trappe, where the famous abbot de Rancé has introduced the reform in the 17th Century, have experienced a long exodus in Europe, going as far as Russia, before returning to England and France, while other branches set off for the United States. From 1813 onwards, Trappist monasteries reopen their doors. We have to wait until 1833 for Benedictine life to begin again at Solesmes and until 1853 for it to be inaugurated at la Pierre-qui-Vire. In both cases they begin from scratch. The same intuition of the importance of monasticism and of its irreplaceable role in the life of the Church animated both Dom Prosper Guéranger (1805–1875) and Dom Jean-Baptiste Muard (1809–1854), even if their approach is quite different: more intellectual and liturgical for the restorer of Solesmes, more ascetic and apostolic for the founder of la Pierrre-qui-Vire.

Dom Prosper Guéranger dates his call to restore the grace of Benedictine life to the Church in France from his priestly ordination and a pilgrimage to the ruins of Marmoutiers, the monastery of the great Saint Martin. He soon acquires the disused monastery of Solesmes, on the banks of the Sarthe very near his native village, and begins to live there according to the *Rule* of Saint Benedict on 11th July 1833. Dom Guéranger knows and admires the great work of the Benedictines of the congregation of Saint-Maur, also called Maurists, who, in the 17th and 18th Centuries made the Parisian Abbey of Saint-Germain-des-Prés a centre of patristic and historical learning. He is even more aware of the eminent place monks have held in the history of the Church, from the deserts of Egypt to the finest hours of Cluny and of Helfta. He is imbued with the importance of prayer, especially liturgical prayer, to which the monasteries give fullness of expression by their fidelity in undertaking the complete cycle of the hours of the divine office.

Thus, for him, the monastery is, above all, a community dedicated to the service of the prayer of the Church. Dom Guéranger's liturgical works contribute decisively to bringing the dioceses of France back to the Roman liturgy. In particular, his work *The Liturgical Year* educates people in a new sensitivity and a deeper knowledge of liturgical prayer, with a view to making possible what the teaching of the popes, from Saint Pius X onwards, will call the "active participation" of the faithful in the mysteries which render glory to God and sanctify them.

Dom Guéranger proposes to monks, oblates (lay people who are spiritually associated with monasteries), and to all those who read *The Liturgical Year*, that they learn to pray by taking part in the prayer of the Church. There is just the right tone, a soundness of doctrine, a perfection of expression and an inimitable "unction" in the formulæ of the prayers of the Roman Church. She has received a special grace from the Holy Spirit to express her hope and give utterance to her contemplation. By making the prayers inspired by the Holy Spirit in the Psalms, the prayers for the Mass and all the other parts of the liturgical cycle her own, the soul puts itself into the hands of the most reliable guide to touch the Heart of God and to receive his graces of light and love.

With this liturgical spirituality Dom Guéranger promotes an understanding of the Church seen as the continuation of the redemptive Incarnation. For liturgical prayer is an ecclesiology in act. The Church can be defined as the people of God in prayer, who, united with her great High

Priest, Christ, renders glory to God and intercedes for the world. The liturgy is offered to monks and nuns as the formative source of their contemplative life and the pledge of their inclusion in the mystery of the Church. The liturgical movement and the ecclesial renewal of the end of the 19th and beginning of the 20th Centuries are in the direct line of the intuitions and works of the Abbot of Solesmes.

> [The novices] will love the Psalms which were the daily nourishment of the saints of our order, convinced that as they become familiar with reciting them they will have made a great step forward in the path that leads to contemplation. They will gently strive to discover the allusions the Holy Church makes in the liturgical texts, in order to nourish themselves on this hidden manna which strengthens the soul even as it enables her to comprehend the things of God.[6]

Dom Marmion or Life in Christ

The entrance of the twenty seven year old Irish priest at Maredsous in Belgium in 1886, fulfils his long held desire. Nevertheless, it is very difficult for him at first, between learning French (even though this had been his mother's native language) and all the deprivations of novitiate life, of which he was spared none. Soon after solemn profession Dom Columba Marmion (1858–1923) can resume his preaching ministry—he is remarkable for his eloquence. Sent in 1899 to the foundation of Mont-César in Louvain, he becomes its first prior. He teaches theology there, uniting sound doctrine with clarity of expression, and constantly applying the truths of the faith to Christian life. In 1909, he is elected abbot of Maredsous. He subsequently

---

[6]   Dom Guéranger, *On the Religious Life* (1885).

spends the hard war years in England and Ireland, before returning to Belgium where he dies in 1923.

During all these years he is an indefatigable retreat preacher and spiritual director, outstanding in the care of souls. He also keeps up a vast correspondence. With the help of a secretary, he becomes a prolific writer having a considerable influence in religious circles. In Dom Marmion, it is first of all his tone that differs from the ambient piety. As a good disciple of Saint Benedict, he is nourished by the liturgy and the Bible, by the Fathers of the Church, by theologians, above all Saint Thomas, and by the great spiritual authors, in particular Saint Francis de Sales.

Blessed Dom Marmion places Christ at the centre of the Christian life and invites the soul to detach itself from that preoccupation with self which prevents us from giving ourselves to God. He draws all its consequences from the Incarnation and from its prolongation in the sacramental life of the Church, the Mystical Body of Christ, as well as in the life of every soul. The Christian is an adopted son of the Father. He has free access to the Father. He has all the privileges of the Son. The spiritual life consists in developing the filial life sown at Baptism, nourished by liturgical life and flowering in the life of love for God, in prayer and sacrifice, and in love for neighbour. Dom Marmion sets forth this classic doctrine, at once both Pauline and Benedictine, in an amiable and persuasive way. He has the art of leading souls and drawing them into the realm of trust and love where he himself habitually lives.

> Christianity is the love of God manifested to the world through Christ, and all our religion ought to be resumed in contemplating this love in Christ, and in responding to the love of Christ so that we may thereby attain to God. Now, the essential attitude that this Divine plan requires of us is that

of adopted children. We still remain beings drawn out of nothing, and before this Father of an incommensurable majesty we ought to cast ourselves down in humblest reverence; but to these fundamental relations which arise from our conditions as creatures, are superimposed, not to destroy but to crown them, relations infinitely higher, wider and more intimate which result from our divine adoption, that are all summed up in the service of God through love.[7]

Thomas Merton or The Paths of Freedom

The monastic life spread to the New World with the arrival of European missionaries and colonists. Although there exist Benedictine foundations in South America from the 16th Century, we have to wait until the beginning of the 19th Century to see the appearance of the first Benedictine and Trappist monasteries in the United States. They then expand there enormously. It is thus that the first American Trappist monastery is founded in 1848, at Gethsemane in Kentucky, by a group of forty three monks who come from the Abbey of Melleray (France). It develops rapidly and is responsible for several foundations in other states.

In 1941, a young American, born in France and educated chiefly in England, enters Gethsemane after having taught for three years at a university. He soon receives the monastic habit and the name of Brother Louis, although he remains better known by the name of Thomas Merton (1915–1968). The young novice, a convert to Catholicism since 1938, embraces the monastery's austere observance with ardour. His superiors quickly recognise his exceptional qualities and his literary talents. He is asked in

---

[7]   Dom Marmion, *Christ in His Mysteries* (1919).

particular to translate the Cistercian authors and to write historical biographies to make the Order known.

His autobiography *The Seven Story Mountain* is published in 1948. It soon becomes a best seller, translated into several languages. In it, Merton describes his personal path, marked by early bereavements, a very liberal education in an independent artistic environment, the disorders of a licentious young student, travel, and meeting prominent individuals, the slow return to his childhood faith, the discovery of Catholicism and his attraction for the contemplative life. This "history of a soul" marries perfectly with the story of the "great generation" of Americans born between the two wars. It is a huge success and turns many young people towards the monastic life.

Thomas Merton subsequently continues to divide his time between his responsibility for monastic formation and an intense literary life. He publishes numerous books on monastic life and contemplative prayer, as well as spiritual biographies. From the sixties, when he is set up in a hermitage near the monastery, he goes on keeping an important diary, writes poetry, and begins to be passionately involved in the causes of peace, ecumenism and eastern religions. He is on a journey in the Far East when he dies accidentally in 1968. His bibliography contains over sixty titles, five volumes of correspondence and the seven volumes of his diary. He is considered by many as a spiritual master.

Thomas Merton's monastic path has been both a descent into the depths of the encounter with God, by means of silence and prayer, and an ever wider openness to the movements of the Spirit in the life and cultures of world religions. He has brilliantly illustrated the contemporary relevance of monastic life according to the *Rule* of Saint Benedict and contributed to opening up the monastic world to universal perspectives in the cultural and moral upheaval of the sixties and the beginnings of globalisation.

> The perfect Christian is not one who is necessarily impeccable and beyond all moral weakness; but he is one who, because his eyes are enlightened to know the full dimensions of the mercy of Christ, is no longer troubled by the sorrows and frailties of this present life. His confidence in God is perfect, because he "knows", so to speak, by experience that God cannot fail him (and yet this knowledge is simply a dimension of a loyal faith). He responds to the mercy of God with perfect trust. For such men, true lovers of God, all things, whether they appear good or evil, are in actuality good. All things manifest the loving mercy of God. All things enable them to grow in love. All events serve to unite them more closely to God. God has turned even obstacles into means to their ends, which are also his own. This is the meaning of "spiritual perfection", and it is attained not by those who have superhuman strength but by those who, though weak and defective in themselves, trust perfectly in the love of God.[8]

Henri Le Saux or Interreligious Encounter

In 1948, Dom Henri Le Saux (1910–1973) leaves Kergonan, a small monastery of the Solesmes Congregation, to answer a call to join Father Jules Monchanin in India. The Breton monk aims to contribute to the encounter with the Indian people, by offering them the monastic life in the school of Saint Benedict. The two Frenchmen found an ashram in which they hope to be able to adopt certain Indian religious customs. It is a question of attracting

---

[8]   Thomas Merton, *Life and Holiness* (1963).

Indians, a deeply religious people, to the Church by
proclaiming Christ to them through the silent preaching
of a contemplative, liturgical and community life.

   Little by little, the original project changes. Vocations
are few and no candidate perseveres. Father Monchanin
dies in 1957. Dom Le Saux realises that an encounter with
India is only possible if he agrees to share the Hindu
religious path from the inside, by study and above all by
pratice. His encounter with spiritual masters, his pilgrim-
ages to the holy places of Hinduism, his study of sacred
documents, especially the *Upanishads*, gradually draw him
towards a more and more solitary way of life. Keeping one
foot in the ashram in Southern India, he spends long
periods in the North, near the Ganges and the Himalayas.
He then treads a sometimes divided spiritual path with on
the one hand his fidelity to the faith and prayer of the
Church, and on the other his engagement with the way of
Hinduism. From the nineteen sixties, he enters into
dialogue with numerous communities of Catholic women,
but also with theologians of various Christian denomina-
tions who share his fascination with the spiritual and
mystical riches of Indian religion.

   Towards the end of his life, when he has the joy of
forming a disciple in whom he recognises a successor, he
achieves an inner reconciliation and is able to live Chris-
tian-Hindu dialogue in a harmonious way. Numerous
books and articles, a vast correspondence and a personal
diary have accompanied this unusual spiritual path. Dom
Le Saux lives this inter-religious dialogue in the depths of
his heart as a fulfilment of his life as a Benedictine monk.
Did not this have its origins at Subiaco, in the cave where
Benedict gave himself up alone to the Alone? It is as a
disciple of the patriarch of monks in the West that he has
come to encounter India, and has placed all that his

monastic formation has given him at the service of one of the major issues of the contemporary world: inter-religious encounter.

> What we need, you see, are Christian monks who have understood the secret of the interior, for they alone will be able to make Hindus understand that Christianity is a matter of the interior and not just a matter of organisation.
>
> Go right down to the depths where there is no longer anything but Him. You have to gaze at Him so intensely that in this gaze there is no longer anything but the One gazed upon. As long as you think you are looking at Him, you are still to the side of Him. Look at Him so hard that there is only Him. Whatever work you are doing, in the office or the kitchen, in the bath or at meditation, there is only the Lord who hears the Father saying: "My child" and Him answering: "My Father". The depths of the soul given, that is all that matters.[9]

The Monks of Tibhirine or Presence until Martyrdom

The foundation of Our Lady of Atlas dates from 1937, three years after the arrival of the founding group in Algeria. If the monastery narrowly escapes being closed at the time of Algerian independence, the direction of its founding takes a new orientation from it. The monks understand that they are called to prayer amidst others who pray. The community gradually comes to consist of monks who feel they have a vocation to be a Christian presence in a Muslim land. The election of Père Christian de Chergé as superior, in 1984, signals greater openness to the local community and a dialogue of work and fraternity with the villagers, while Brother Luke's dispen-

---

[9]   Henri Le Saux, *Letters to Sœur Marie-Thérèse Le Saux, OSB.*

sary welcomes everyone without discrimination. At this period the monks define themselves thus: "Guests of the Algerian people, who are virtually all Muslims, these brothers would like to contribute to witnessing that peace between peoples is a gift that God makes to men of all places and times, and that it is for believers, here and now, to show this inalienable gift. They do so by their mutual respect and by supporting and challenging one another in a spirit of healthy and fruitful emulation."

The political change of 1989 alters the country's equilibrium and provides more extremist Muslims with the opportunity to make their voice heard in the elections. Even if the monks preserve good relations with their neighbourhood, the general situation deteriorates. Attacks multiply, aimed in particular against Christians. In 1993, twelve Christians at a nearby building site are assassinated. Should the monks leave like several other male and female religious? Reflecting prayerfully together leads them to make a bold and dangerous choice. They will stay, in order to give witness of being a presence which seeks the good whatever the cost.

One night in March 1996, a group from the GIA breaks in and takes seven monks away as prisoners.[10] On the 21st May following it is learned that they have been assassinated. Their heads, cut off after their deaths, are found, recognised and buried. They are beatified on 8th December 2018 among the nineteen Martyrs of Algeria.

Presence to the point of the supreme gift of self: can there exist a more perfect imitation of Christ? The monks

[10]   An Islamic extremist group, the GIA (Armed Islamic Group) aimed to overthrow the secular Algerian regime and replace it with an Islamic state. The GIA began its violent activity in 1992 after Algiers voided the victory of the Islamic Salvation Front—the largest Islamic opposition party—in the first round of legislative elections in December 1991.

of Tibhirine went into a deeper, truly divine, region of freedom to look for the humble strength to give their lives, to allow themselves to be taken by an "enemy" whom they refused to consider other than as a brother. They received the grace of martyrdom on the soil of the African continent that had seen the first monks take the path of the desert in order to imitate the martyrs in total gift and love without limits.

> If one day—and that could be today—I become the victim of the terrorism which now seems to want to include all the foreigners living in Algeria, I would like my community, my Church and my family to remember that my life was GIVEN to God and to this country. May they accept that the One Master of all life cannot be indifferent to this brutal departure. Let them pray for me: how would I ever be found worthy of such an offering? Let them know how to associate this death with so many equally violent ones overlooked in the indifference of anonymity. [...] And you also, the friend of my last moments, who will not know what you are doing. Yes, I want to THANK YOU too, and to say ADIEU. And may it be given to us to meet again, blessed thieves, in Paradise, please God, the Father of us both. AMEN! Insha'Allah![11]

A Family Spirit

At the end of this rapid overview, the Benedictine Family is seen as both very varied and very unified. Over the course of the centuries the Holy Spirit has displayed in the sons and daughters of Saint Benedict the infinite possibilities of charity. In particular, He has raised up spiritual masters and examples of sanctity who assure the continu-

---

[11] Dom Christian De Chergé, *Testament*.

ity and constant renewal of monastic grace in the church. Thanks to them, armies of anonymous monks and nuns, but also a great number of lay people, affiliated with the Benedictine Order by oblation or by ties of friendship with this or that monastery, are daily stimulated, enlightened and encouraged to respond to the call of Christ who fixes His gaze on each one of us saying: "Follow me!".

With remarkable flexibility, the Benedictine family has been able to integrate the contribution of numerous spiritual currents subsequent to St Benedict. It is thus, for example, that the sacramental grace and ecclesial vision of Cluny, the Marian and mystical inspiration of Clairvaux, the more subjective devotion of the modern era with its meditation exercises, its science of prayer and sense of adoration, the "little way" of Sainte Thérèse and openness to the missions and to other world religions have been able to find a place and even flower in a Benedictine setting. Monasticism can welcome and be nourished by them because, basically, it is less a specialised spiritual school than the search for the full flowering of the grace of our baptism. "A school of the Lord's service" (Prologue 45), "a school of charity" (Saint Bernard), a school of sanctity, Benedictine monasticism is careful to listen to what the Spirit says to the churches. It does not confine itself to one particular spiritual path. It makes us open to the action of the Spirit, who draws all the faithful to sanctity. It offers not so much a method as a nourishing foundation for the Christian life, and it is in this way that it is capable of sustaining and inspiring all forms of life and commitment.

3 LIVING IN THE WORLD ACCORDING TO THE SPIRIT OF SAINT BENEDICT

I S IT POSSIBLE for us to be included among those who follow in the footsteps of these great witnesses to the Benedictine tradition? Can an ordinary Christian life, occupied with family and social duties, lend itself to an adaptation of instructions drawn up for those living in the cloister? How can we benefit from Saint Benedict's wisdom in our daily lives? How are we to approach this holiness, the path to which he showed so many men and women, disciples of his life and of his *Rule*? How are we to go about it? Where do we begin? What could I introduce into my daily life? To what could I be more attentive? Where should my priorities be? The following pages are an attempt to outline an answer to these questions. Let each reader be attentive to what the Spirit suggests to him or her.

Starting from the Liturgy

When he organises the life of the monastery, Saint Benedict quite naturally makes his own the framework of liturgical prayer. This gives a rhythm and orientation to time. However important the place where the monastery is situated may be, with its qualities of solitude, silence and separation from the world, time is even more important. It is the rhythm of choral prayer, with its seven daily gatherings to which is added the night Vigil, that determines the length and structures the time. In the liturgy, the people of God in prayer receives its unity from its orientation towards God. Benedictine spirituality, from its point of departure, thus invites us to move away from our self-centredness in order to join a people in prayer. It is there, at the heart of the spiritual network of the Mystical Body of Christ, that we have access to the wellspring of the Spirit.

Whoever wants to draw inspiration from the *Rule* will thus do well to begin by setting in place a rule of prayer. This can vary in accordance with the availability and duties of each person. The Mass is central. Sunday Mass of course, but why not include Mass in my daily schedule several times in the week, or better still, every day? The Eucharistic celebration is the source and summit of the Church's life. To take part in it is to be nourished daily on the Word of life and on the Bread of life. By beginning with the liturgy we anchor our spiritual life in the prayer of the Church. The Church is a community of people who pray, a society of divine praise and intercession.

Saint Benedict did not linger over long theological considerations on the central place of the liturgy in the Christian life. It was enough for him to invite his disciples to give it first place concretely: "Let nothing be preferred to the Work of God".[1] This must also be the attitude of whoever wants to be his disciple. To enter into the spirit of the *Rule* is to begin to enter into the liturgy. Very soon, the need to return to liturgical prayer during the day will be felt. Whether I adopt the Liturgy of the Hours or chose a more or less adapted form of the Benedictine Office, morning prayer (Lauds) and evening prayer (Vespers or Compline) can become a simple and ecclesial way of balancing my day. Liturgical time, with its cycle, and saints' feastdays then begin to take on form. This gives a profound

---

[1]   RB 43, 2.

direction to life, orienting all activity, personal and ecclesial, towards Christ. "We look forward to His coming in glory": this phrase from the Creed expresses well the general meaning which Christ gives to human time. He reigns over our existence, which is ultimately determined in relation to Him. All human time moves towards Christ, who comes to us in a perpetual Advent, through the mysteries of the Incarnation and Redemption that the liturgy celebrates, as well as through the veneration of the Saints. This orientation towards the Lord of time and history puts the other levels of our life in perspective.

The disciple of Saint Benedict keeps watch with the Church. He awaits the Lord's second coming and this is the source of his profound peace. Thus he avoids being confined to a purely earthly horizon. He keeps watch in hope because he understands that Christ is at work in the dough of human history. He is united with His action by the intercession, contemplation and praise which spring forth from the constant celebration of the paschal mystery. In the twelfth degree of humility the monk already sees himself under the judgement of God.[2] Under the eyes of a judge who is also a merciful saviour, he is aware of the sinful dimensions of his life. Little by little, this practice of always placing his life under the gaze of Christ who is coming (we can think here of the Christ Pantocrator whose representation in the apse of Byzantine Churches dominates the whole edifice) becomes habitual in the person who regularly participates in the mysteries which the Church constantly celebrates in her liturgy. Even under the very humble form of an office recited silently in the quiet of one's room or with the help of a media app in the anonymity of travelling by public transport, the liturgy puts us into the presence of Christ who prays in His

---

[2]   RB 7, 64.

Church. It opens the soul to the action of Christ's Spirit. It imperceptibly forms and transforms us. It harmonises us with Christ. It evangelises the whole person: the soul, with its capacities of thought and affection; the body with its senses open to creation; the psychological depths criss-crossed by all sorts of desires; and the depth of the heart where God dwells.

The desire to pray at night may also arise, this vigil with the Church waiting for the Beloved. Certain circumstances, the vigils of great feasts, key moments in the liturgical year, are good opportunities to try this. As Saint Benedict explains in the chapter on the dormitory, it is a matter of being "always ready", of living in the spirit of vigilance and hope of Advent, with a purified desire totally centred on Christ.[3]

Yield yourself with confidence to the Church's great movement of prayer, Saint Benedict is still saying to us today: Christ will become the light for your steps.

Living in the Presence of God

With the early Christians and the desert monks, Benedict is convinced of the divine omnipresence and how that affects the way we live. The spiritual life, the life orientated towards God, cannot simply be a question of regular prayer times. Our entire existence unfolds before the Lord's eyes. He watches the children of men with the untiring interest of a very loving Father. He sounds the depths of His creature. He knows his heart. He decodes his thoughts. He listens to his desires.

In biblical tradition, taking into account God's loving attention has received the name of "the fear of God". Monks have always accorded it extreme importance. It is not a

---

[3]   Cf. RB 22, 6.

question of being frightened of God, but of having a refined awareness of His presence to all that we are and all that we do. It originates not so much in experience, for the divine presence is not usually perceptible to the senses, as in an act of faith: "We believe", writes Saint Benedict, "that God is present everywhere and is always beholding the good and the wicked".[4] It is up to us to choose: we can ignore this presence, forget it, disregard it; but we can also recognise it, take it seriously and draw consequences from it.

In the first degree of humility, the monk flees forgetfulness.[5] He ceaselessly remembers that God sees him, that he lives under his gaze, that his actions and intentions are observed, examined and weighed by a God who is both supremely loving and supremely exigent—supremely exigent because He is love. The repeatedly renewed awareness of this fundamental dimension of our existence causes our very being to shudder, less out of fright than out of "reverence", another word dear to Saint Benedict. To revere is to have a sense of the mystery. Divine love which penetrates and dwells in all things is supremely worthy of that respectful attention which we give to important and great things. The fear of God ensures that we are not alone with our consciousness, still less alone in the world, but according to the old monastic expression: "alone with the Alone", namely in a constant relationship with the One who is the home and centre of reality: the thrice holy God.

Can we learn to live thus in the presence of God? A comparison may perhaps help. We learn to live in God's presence as we enter into a friendship. It is basically a matter of opening up little by little to Love, which is the key to our existence. In the monastery, space is entirely

---

[4]   RB 19, 1
[5]   RB 7, 10–30.

organised so as to help us live in the presence of God. The places, persons, the rhythm, words, meetings, activities all orient us towards God in one way or another. In the same way, may those who live in the world become sensitive to the divine presence. Let them have recourse to the symbols that remind them of it. A cross on the wall, an icon on the desk, the church in the village, a rosary in the pocket, the medal of Saint Benedict or of the Blessed Virgin can all become so many very simple, every-day signs helping me to remain in the presence of God, or to return to it when I have slightly lost sight of it. Exterior signs sustain the attention of my heart as it gradually becomes more spiritually sensitive. Little by little I learn to keep watch with a flexible and constant attention. Everywhere, at every moment, I can be in contact with God. It is not a matter of straining to be in constant communication with Him (that is for the Angels), but of allowing a habitual feeling of divine companionship to grow. God is the eye which is always looking at me with love, the hand which is protecting me, the shade sheltering me, the light enlightening me, the warmth comforting me, the freshness soothing me. Living in His presence means learning to yield myself to His Holy Spirit. His varied action, reaching into the intimate depths of myself and ever drawing me further beyond myself, guides my entire life. Then the street or the town become a cloister, each meeting a visitation, each face an icon. God's presence must first be recognised and honoured before it can be served. There is a Benedictine grace which consists of honouring the presence of God. It implies a contemplation which precedes, and is the foundation for, all that I could try to do for Him.

Saint Benedict is still saying to us today, be united, in the silence of the heart, with the God who is the guest of your soul and the attentive, benevolent observer of your whole existence.

Working for the Glory of God

According to a phrase which, even if it only dates from the 19th Century, still provides a felicitous synthesis, the monk prays and works: *Ora et labora*. This expression has almost become a second motto of the Benedictine Order, after the famous *Pax*. It reflects well a concern for alternating activities and maintaining a balance which does, in fact, go back to the origins of monasticism. It is not possible to be always at prayer or adoration. We have to live and for that we have to work. The monastic vocation does not dispense us from taking our part in the toil by which man brings into subjection the earth, serving the Creator's plan and winning his bread by the sweat of his brow. In a society where slavery is still widespread, Benedict does not hesitate to foresee for all the monks participation in the manual activities linked to community life, both in the workshops and in the fields. "They will be truly monks if they live by the labour of their hands, as our fathers and the apostles".[6] To the craftsmen of the monastery, he gives an order which says a great deal about the orientation of our whole life towards worship: "That in all things God may be glorified".[7] This concerns as much the quality of the work as its selling price. What we do is to be done well, it is to be useful and beautiful, and as far as possible, it must be less expensive, so as to be accessible to the poorest.

A real work ethic is being sketched in the background. This is simply Christian. A "Benedictine work" is not first and foremost the painstaking work of erudition that this

---

[6]   RB 48, 8.
[7]   RB 57, 9.

expression has evoked since the learned labours of the monks of Saint-Germain-des Prés in the 17th and 18th Centuries. It is a work well thought out and well done, a good work in every aspect. Over the centuries monks have undertaken and continue to undertake the most varied works: agriculture and craft work, fine arts, medicine and education, commerce and industrial or technical services, theological, literary or scientific studies, to say nothing of the ministries associated with the priesthood such as catechesis, spiritual accompaniment, evangelisation or missionary work. They have often experienced great success. Sometimes the fortunes they have made have contributed to the hastening of their decadence.

In the school of Saint Benedict, then, let us give the hours of work their full value. Work is offered in advance during morning prayer, just as it is also presented to God in the evening office. It is done in a climate of the fear of God, under the gaze of him for whose glory we carry out all our works, however modest they may be. Sometimes we can be not totally immersed in an activity, so that our heart remains available for a silent dialogue of love with the Lord. More often, however, the context of the work as well as its nature, require all our attention: to people, to ideas and to things to be done. Just as we can usually pray better in a silent chapel, but can, with a little practice, converse with God amidst the crowds and noise of the underground, so we can all learn to remain gently in contact with God even amidst the most urgent activities. It is not a matter of escaping from a work which is seen only as a necessary evil, but of living the covenant dimension which characterises the whole Christian life. I am working for God, because I offer Him what I do. But I am also working with God, who gives me His light and His strength. So it is that I serve God in my brethren, in joy and freedom of soul, in a climate of peace and in a spirit of prayer.

Sharing the fruits of our labour in some way with those who are in need also forms part of the Christian attitude to work. Sharing what we do not need is always a rule. Depriving ourselves even of what seems to be necessary can sometimes be required, as it was in Saint Benedict's day, when a famine ravaged Campania. Whoever gives to the poor receives abundantly from the very hand of God, as is demonstrated by Saint Benedict's miracle of an oil barrel filling up after a beggar had been given the monastery's last bottle of oil.[8]

Also very typical of the Benedictine spirit is a dimension of beauty in the work accomplished. There is, first of all, the elementary beauty of a work well done. In certain areas, it is possible to let the work blossom, with that distinctive freedom and fullness designated by the Beautiful. While it is important to beware of aestheticism, which traps one into the search for beauty and makes of art, the artist and the work of art potential idols, it remains true that the pursuit of a simple and noble beauty is a characteristic component of Benedictine work. Anyone who has visited a medieval Cistercian abbey such as Sénanque, Clairmont or Pontigny, or who allowed himself to be uplifted by the movement and purity of a Gregorian melody, understands the powerfully inspiring force of simple, perfectly modulated forms, and penetrates directly into Saint Benedict's spirit of work.

In your work, Saint Benedict is still saying to us today, remain in the presence of your God, live out your marriage bond with Him, share what you have with your brethren and accomplish a work of beauty.

---

[8]   Cf. *Life*, ch. 29.

Putting Oneself at the Service of One's neighbour

One of a monk's characteristics is his availability for
whatever obedience asks of him. He has renounced his
own will.[9] He is available, ready to be sent here or there,
according to need. He is not hindered by any personal
objectives, a career plan or a fortune to make. He gave up
everything when he pronounced his vows[10] and each day
strips himself of whatever is liable to weigh him down, so
that he is free to serve wherever God Himself, through his
superiors, is calling him. Thus his life takes on the form of
service: service of God in the liturgy, service of the community in the daily tasks, service of all his brothers and
sisters in humanity by the gift of himself, which he strives
to practice in all things.

In organising the life of the monastery, Saint Benedict
gives an important symbolic place to the kitchen service.[11]
All must do it, except those who are too weak or really too
busy. The servers begin and end their week of service in
the oratory of the monastery recommending themselves
to the prayer of all. On Saturday evening they participate
in the washing of the feet of the whole community, a
conceivable enough hygienic service in antiquity, but
above all one which repeats Our Lord's gesture of washing
the feet of His disciples. By underlining the importance of
this service, Saint Benedict invites the monk to make his
whole life a service of God and his brothers in imitation
of Christ the Servant.

This has important consequences. It is always a person
that I serve. Service puts me in a relationship with another,
whose needs I serve and whose dignity I honour. Service,

---

[9]   RB 5, 7–9.
[10] RB 58, 24–25.
[11] RB 35.

says Benedict, increases charity. We are to understand that it fosters communion among persons. It puts what is done for one or several of the brethren at the service of the communion of all in love. It puts people first. It is for them and in relation to them that we do this or that. Thus a fine cake, which the austere Benedict might perhaps have been surprised to see appear on the monks' table on a solemnity, is not only a beautiful and good work done for the glory of God, it is an honour rendered to those people who enter into this privileged form of communion expressed in the feast.

The *Rule* was adopted partly because of its merciful attention to individual people which is one of its dominant characteristics. This is expressed in every way: when it prescribes before everything attention to the sick,[12] but also attention to each brother according to his age, his health, what he can and cannot do, his bodily and spiritual needs, his physical and psychological character.[13] The *Rule* leans kindly over the youngest and the old, adapting for them the measure of food and of fasting.[14] In the reception of guests it reminds us to pay special attention to the poorest.[15] The cellarer, the infirmarian, the novice master and the guest master are all servants who exemplify the service of each individual which is at the heart of the abbot's mission.[16]

The *Rule* thus strongly challenges all Christians by inviting them to see their lives from the angle of service. Equally remote from *servility*, which would lower my dignity, and from an unbridled striving for a position of *domination* where I would be trying to put others at my

---

[12]   RB 36, 1.
[13]   Cf. RB 2, 31–32 and *passim.*
[14]   RB 37.
[15]   RB 53, 15.
[16]   Cf. RB 2, 37.

service, compassionate *service* of others gives each one his right place. This attitude springs from a perspective inspired by faith. It is Christ whom we serve in the least of His brethren, according to the teaching in the parable of the last judgement in Saint Matthew (cf. Mt 25: 31–46). The preferential love for Christ, which runs through the whole *Rule*, is thus especially expressed in the care we give to our neighbour, in his weaknesses and his needs. This begins in the circle of those nearest to us, gradually expanding towards those whom the Lord sends to us and whom He asks us to serve with patience, gentleness and humble charity, full of compassion. It might seem utopian, and perhaps dangerous, to place service at the heart of commerce and city. Yet it is probably here that can be found one of the most important contributions of the spirit of Benedictine monasticism to the right ordering of political life.

To reign with Christ the King, Saint Benedict is still saying to us today, take the path of serving others and imitate Christ the Servant.

Constant Conversion

By declaring that Lent is a privileged time of the year for a monk, the one that should ideally set the tone for the whole of his life, Saint Benedict makes conversion a permanent dimension of our existence.[17] There are special times for purification of the heart, such as Lent and Advent, but there are no real holidays from it. Whoever applies himself attentively to the rhythms of the liturgical year is stimulated on his path towards sanctity in a way that is both flexible and regular. On a personal level, having frequent recourse to the Sacrament of Reconcilia-

---

[17]   Cf. RB 49, 1.

tion, and extending it by opening one's heart to a spiritual father, are important stages on the path to docility to the Holy Spirit's inspirations. In the same vein, one may feel the need to go on retreat in a Benedictine or Cistercian monastery, at regular intervals (often annual).

Saint Benedict knows that the path to holiness is long and that progress is rarely spectacular. By the vow of stability,[18] he invites the monk to provide himself with means of persevering in his intention of conversion. He knows that our enemies are many. Boredom, discouragement, sadness, sometimes even despair can easily interfere and eventually halt our progress. We can be tempted to go to look elsewhere, to change our spiritual father or even our spiritual path. A lot of time is sometimes wasted avoiding serious conversion in this way. Often, we are simply asked to carry on, to persevere, to hold on somehow, in spite of falls or lack of apparent progress. The spiritual combat is lived out in time. It aims to strengthen in us constancy in our orientation towards Christ, constancy which includes the fidelity of setting out again each day along the path of evangelical holiness.

Saint Benedict places at the end of his list of tools of good works a golden rule: "Never to despair of God's mercy".[19] In this way he indicates the source of our perseverance: it is not found in a stiffening of the will, but in looking with confidence and love towards the God of mercy revealed in Jesus Christ. In this way, joy is guaranteed. There is a profound joy in beginning again each morning, as after each Mass or after each confession, with a new energy which springs neither from a naive optimism nor from an effort of self will, but from a renewed encounter with the God of mercy upon whom I ground my life. Desert monasticism

---

[18] Cf. RB 58, 9.15.17.
[19] RB 4, 74.

soon realised that the decisive element in conversion is not that of ascetic achievement, but the liberation brought about when I willingly recognise that deep down I am a sinner and thus entirely dependent on divine mercy. The portrait of the monk who has arrived at the summit of humility is provided for us by the publican in the Gospel who does not dare to raise his eyes to heaven and who confesses his sin.[20] To whoever might be tempted to see in the publican someone cramped and guilt ridden, Jesus replies that it is indeed he who is "justified" by God, and not the one who uses his spiritual accomplishments as a pretext for secretly despising others. He who humbles himself is lifted up. The sinner who confesses his fault is not only forgiven but filled with light and strength by divine charity, which renders him capable of carrying out his daily actions within the ambiance of divine love, and thus of "covering a multitude of sins" (1 Pet 4, 8).

The path of conversion is a path of humility. In it I discover ever more clearly the depth of my sin. I become more aware of the gravity of sin as an offence against God. In doing this I imperceptibly draw nearer to the holiness of God. This cannot be achieved by my good works. It is a gift of grace, a present of mercy. If fidelity to this work of conversion normally leads us to greater self-mastery and to progress in virtue, it is also accompanied by a keener awareness of the gratuity of grace. Our response to the gift of God, who mercifully offers us His love, can only be the humble confession of our faults and the grateful praise of His mercy. Benedictine holiness develops into a celebration of divine mercy. A celebration in the liturgy, of course, but also in the constant praise of the heart, which thirsts to celebrate for ever the mercies of the

---

[20]   RB 7, 65.

Lord: "Give thanks to the Lord, for He is good, for His mercy endures for ever".[21]

Persevere and don't give up, Saint Benedict is still saying to us today, and do not be surprised that you need conversion every day; walk, full of hope, along the paths of mercy.

Loving Humbly

The *Rule* of Saint Benedict certainly cannot make any exclusive claims on humility or charity, which are at the heart of Christian ethics. Nevertheless, the *Rule* does articulate these two key virtues in its own special way. In practice, humility and charity flow from the service of God, in praise, and from the service of others, in compassion. They spring from the same love for Christ which inspires us to glorify the Father and to serve our neighbour.

Here, our Benedictine and monastic attention looks toward purity of heart. How can I love my brother if my heart is full of myself? How can I serve him and feel compassion for his needs? In the battle against the passions which enslave the sinner's heart, the tradition represented by Saint Benedict is centred on overcoming pride. Many other inclinations can paralyse the exercise of the gift of charity, poured into our hearts at baptism. Without being unaware of them, Benedict goes straight to the root of the soul's ills. Pride is the great enemy, because it lulls us into the illusion that we have no need of the spiritual physician, and that we can advance towards our perfection by our own strength. Humility, however, opens our hearts to the divine light by the exercise of the gift of fear. It provides protection from the illusions of self-will, by subjecting a monk to his abbot by the bond of

---

[21]   Cf. RB 7, 46.

obedience. It leads us to accept the place of mediation, human and ecclesial, which flows from the redemptive Incarnation. It makes us follow Christ along the path of obedience. It gives meaning to humiliating circumstances, and allows us to welcome them as so many graces conforming us to Christ and giving us spiritual freedom.

I must therefore resolutely choose the place of a disciple in order to learn the art of being humble which leads to the art of loving. The apprenticeship may include the reading of monastic authors, visiting and getting to know a community, the choice of a spiritual father and submission to his advice in a spirit of obedience. Note, however, that it is, above all, a matter of an entirely interior purification of the heart. There can be no question of being satisfied with a purely exterior imitation of monastic ways: it is not a matter of playing at being a monk! I must strive to enter into Saint Benedict's spirit and gradually steep my Christian life in it.

The grace of humility is asked for and cultivated by being attentive to the important dispositions indicated by Saint Benedict in Chapter 7 of his *Rule*: the fear of God and obedience, patience and silence, the acceptance of objectively humiliating circumstances, detachment from whatever puts us forward, makes us stand out, attracts applause and human glory, nourishes vanity and flatters the ego. I am not being asked to renounce the use of my gifts or to refuse to accept important responsibilities if they are laid upon me. But all this must be done in a spirit of service and for the glory of God, seeking self-effacement and discretion.

Furthermore, this concern for humility must not deflect us from its purpose, which is to give us access to a freer and more generous charity.[22] The humble person does not

---

[22]   RB 7, 67.

look at himself, does not blame or congratulate himself, he looks at God and enters more and more into the current of His love. In this love, his life becomes unified. The heart that the Holy Spirit purifies from the sicknesses of soul that are the passions becomes free to love more. We are not so much called to undertake new, more spectacular works of charity as to accomplish all things, even the most ordinary, with an impulse of generosity ever more simple and joyful. Saint Benedict perceives in respect, patience, obedience and forgetfulness of self so many signs of a truly loving heart. It is in this soil that the delicate touches of human affection between couples, brethren and friends can flourish. They are never separated from loving reverence for God and warm affection for Christ in His humanity and His divinity, which the symbol of His adorable Heart unites.[23]

Humble yourself under the mighty hand of God, Saint Benedict is still saying to us today, and He will exalt you by creating in you a heart after His own Heart, a heart which truly loves.

Integral Ecology

In the monastic outlook of a Saint Athanasius of Alexandria († 373), author of the *Life of Saint Anthony*, the monk who draws near to God by a life of asceticism and contemplation gradually recovers his full human dignity. Anthony as an old man seems to his surprised visitors always as young and supple as ever, he radiates light and peace, he reminds them of the native youth of man fresh from the hands of God. At first sight, Saint Benedict offers nothing similar in the *Rule*. In his approach to the Paschal Mystery he remains firmly on the side of Lent and penance. Easter

---

[23]   Cf. RB 72.

and the Resurrection are the object of a wholly spiritual desire.[24] Eternal life increasingly becomes the sole object of a monk's desires.[25] But Benedict does not describe any transformation in the monk himself, who might thereby be, so to speak, already clothed with heavenly light. For him it is enough that his disciples should be fully human. Nevertheless, the *Life* of Saint Benedict seems to suggest that entering by faith into the light of God can make certain people radiate a peace and gentleness which belong to another world. What, then is the Benedictine vision of a humanity reconciled with God?

In this context we must begin with humility. The humanly and spiritually mature person is someone who recognises that he is a sinner, welcomed and saved by divine mercy. Because of this, he becomes free to make of all that he is and all that he does a gift of love. No excessive spiritualisation follows on from this, no "angelism", but an incarnation fully consented to. For Benedict, who once again echoes monastic tradition, the vision of humanity reconciled by encounter with Christ will find a privileged expression in hospitality. The wise old man whom the *Rule* places at the monastery gate is a good, prudent person, full of gentleness and attentiveness. Quite the opposite of a robot or answer-machine, he gives what only a fully developed human being can give. By his whole attitude, he honours the visitor's humanity. He welcomes him, that is to say he honours him, offers him safety and good will, viewing him in the light of God. The visitor who knocks on the door thus finds himself at home because he is with God.[26]

---

[24]   RB 49, 7.
[25]   RB 4, 46.
[26]   Cf. RB 66.

The chapter on the reception of guests[27] describes even more impressively the welcome and temporary incorporation of the one who knocks at the door. The whole community, led by the abbot, comes to meet him. First he is greeted with great humility, going as far as a full prostration. Then they pray together and exchange the kiss of peace. The "divine law" is read to the visitor and his physical needs are attended to: the washing of his feet, food, rest. Special care must be taken of the poor and pilgrims, the most needy guests, and those towards whom one might be inclined to pay less attention than to the rich and powerful.

Hospitality is a fundamental attitude for Benedictines; it is the most visible expression of their service of humanity. Disciples of Christ, true God and true man, monks serve Christ in the guests,[28] that is to say they play their part in giving them honour and take special care of what is most sacred in their dignity. Hospitality mobilises what is best in man, which consists in recognising in each person, known or unknown, someone loved by Christ, saved by His Blood, rich in a supernatural dignity linked to his vocation to salvation and sanctity. Through the abbot and the brethren specifically charged with hospitality, it is the whole community which welcomes the individual who knocks at the door. The community integrates him into the temporary communion, which is like a sacrament of the eternal communion of the divine life, to which we are all called. The monk and his guest thus meet in the light of the One who welcomes them both, Christ, who calls them into the full communion of His filial life with the Father.

---

[27]   RB 53.

[28]   RB 53, 1.

The divine depth of Benedictine hospitality contains a lesson in anthropology as simple as it is fundamental. It demonstrates that man has been created for communion: with his brothers and sisters in humanity, with the cosmos and with his God. There is no situation which can deprive him of his supernatural vocation or of the eminent dignity which this confers upon him. In this context, being inspired by Saint Benedict's spirituality does not mean transforming one's family home into a hotel open to every stranger. It is a question rather of seeing one's family and home as centres of growth and education, where one places oneself at the service of human dignity in a spirit of what recent papal teaching calls "integral ecology". Respect for nature and for life reaches its summit in the honour shown to persons and in the untiring service of their dignity, linked to their divine, eternal vocation. In allowing myself to be awakened to my own dignity by assiduously listening to the Word of God and frequenting the sacraments, I become more capable of fulfilling my vocation as "guardian of my brother" (cf. Gen 4, 9) and "master" of creation (cf. Gen 1, 28). I allow myself to live ever more by the contemplation of Christ, King of the universe and Redeemer of man. In welcoming the poorest of my brothers and entering into communion with him, I discover my authentic identity as "universal brother". Hospitality awakens, as much in the one who gives it as the one who receives it, an awareness of what it means to be truly human. Far from being the condescension of the one who is privileged towards the one who is impoverished, it is the humble service of the other's human dignity, expressed under the sign of sharing and festivity. Now, it is in serving the other in what is most human and most divine in him that we make ourselves more human and become more like God.

The idea of integral ecology expresses well this respect for and this profound understanding of the dignity of all creatures on the many levels of their relationships with each other: biological, economic, political and, crowning everything and giving it meaning and purpose, spiritual (or supernatural). In accordance with his practical genius, Saint Benedict does not elaborate an abstract theory, but shows us how to practise, in a simple way, what will make us deeply human, in touch with the natural and human environment in which we live. He reminds us that being welcoming and hospitable, and thus refusing to exclude others or discriminate, is the path towards the communion of men with one another and their harmonious integration in the universe, at once both material and spiritual, wherein their lives can flourish.

Furthermore, the choice of personal poverty and of sharing our goods makes monasteries places where simplicity and sobriety of life reign, even if their natural setting and architecture are often privileged. The chapters which Saint Benedict devotes to arranging meals and fasting[29], to the distribution of necessary goods[30], to simplicity in dress[31] and, more generally, to the organisation of the monastery as a self-contained and at least partly self-sufficient living space[32], can become a great source of inspiration for many of our concrete attitudes in daily life. A sober life style, including in particular a controlled use of energy and a development of the natural environment respectful of its equilibrium, finds a stimulating model in the *Rule*. Above all, Saint Benedict gives decisive spiritual illumination to this attention to ecology. We are directed

---

[29] RB 39–40.

[30] RB 33–34.

[31] RB 55.

[32] RB 66, 6–7.

to integral ecology, which places at the heart of its preoccupations respect and service of the human person, created in the image of God and for His glory.

Watch over your own humanity, Saint Benedict is still saying to us today, by welcoming your brother and protecting in him the miracle of Life.

Doing All Things with Moderation

"He wrote a rule for monks, outstanding for its discretion and its pleasant style".[33] This verdict of Saint Gregory is justly famous. Benedict is not content to provide the main aspects of the spiritual life such as fear, service, humility or charity. He makes a point of regulating the details of life. The measure of love is loving without measure, according to the well-known saying of Saint Bernard. It is impossible to overdo charity or the good zeal of love. It is also impossible to be too humble—if that adjective really describes the spiritual attitude extolled in Chapter 7 of the *Rule*, and is not merely a psychological characteristic. By contrast, with regard to everything that concerns the means to be used, man needs moderation. He constantly needs to find the balance between too much and too little. It is possible to pray too much, to fast too much, to overdo correction, to expend too much energy. We are often tempted to go all out in a single direction, when life requires that we constantly balance our efforts and activities. So it is that Benedict knows how to draw our attention to complementary poles: prayer and work, silence and singing; separation from the world and hospitality; solitude and common life.

Saint Benedict's practical genius excels in determining a measure that is neither too high, such as the imitation of

---

[33]   *Life*, ch. 36.

certain of the desert Fathers' exploits might suggest,[34] nor too low, such as that with which the decadent monasticism of his day was all too easily satisfied. Twice, Saint Benedict explicitly states that we must "do all things with moderation": in advice given to the cellarer, the abbot's right hand man with regard to material administration,[35] and in advice addressed to the abbot, with regard to the organisation of work.[36] In the latter case, he gives the reason: "because of the weak". In our common life, we do not all have the same strengths or the same aptitudes in every area. So the psalmody, the work, the measure of food and clothing, and a thousand other things, must be regulated in such a way as to provide for everyone. The weakest will not be discouraged and the strong will not be frustrated. Benedict recommends this subtle and demanding balance to the abbot by praising to him the "discretion which is the mother of the virtues".[37] The word discretion here is equivalent to what we might today call prudence, or balance.

It is first of all the *Rule* itself which is evidently prudent, in clearly fixing its objectives and indicating a median measure. But it also leaves many practical decisions to the abbot, who is the sole judge of what is appropriate in the particular circumstances of the monastery, according to his personal prudence. The monk is himself also invited to demonstrate good judgement and discretion. On the one hand, he can be called to give advice on important matters for which the abbot assembles the whole community.[38] On the other hand, so that his obedience is a free act and not simply the execution of an order given to a slave, the monk

---

[34] Cf. RB 18, 25.
[35] RB 31, 12.
[36] RB 48, 9.
[37] RB 64, 19.
[38] RB 3.

must evaluate what he is asked to do. Is he able to obey the order given? Is it difficult? Does it seem impossible? He has to be able to explain the problem to his superior, reasonably and calmly, entering into a constructive dialogue with him.[39] On a practical level, with regard to things that are his responsibility, he has to make judgements about what it is appropriate to do, choose fitting means, adapt to people and circumstances, in short, to exercise discretion.

We may well consider that one of the reasons for the *Rule*'s lasting success is precisely its genius for moderation. It is true that, over the course of the centuries, this quality has lent itself to interpretations that have sometimes been more strict and sometimes more flexible, often enough in reaction to one another. But it remains the case that, in itself, the *Rule* preaches a balance which is an ideal stimulus. Reading and re-reading the *Rule*, we gradually learn to be inspired by its balanced approach to human realities. Benedict was aware of the limits which beset our best intentions. He encourages us to do better, but he reminds us that the path to holiness is a long one. Patience with oneself and with others leads us to restrain anything that might be excessive and, in this sense, too human in our zeal for holiness. Moderation, balance, equilibrium, temperateness are so many words that admirably describe a character which is truly Benedictine and the way of being human which the *Rule* promulgates. Benedict himself moved on from the intransigence of the hermit, so caught up by the absoluteness of his spiritual search that he forgot the date of Easter, to the prudent moderation of the *Rule*, which allows many to tread the path leading to the summits of charity and perfection.[40] A spiritual life inspired by Saint Benedict is certainly marked by this search for moderation

---

[39]   RB 68.
[40]   RB 73, 1.

which little by little establishes the reign of peace. Benedictine *Pax*, this Peace that is the motto of the order of Saint Benedict, is given as a fruit of the Holy Spirit in the soil of order and moderation which the *Rule* puts in place.

In this climate, people flourish. Saint Benedict demonstrates a fine sensitivity to diversity of temperament and character. He gives advice about how to govern that places people at the heart of the micro-society formed by the monastery. All that is done in his community is achieved with people as they are, and in a certain sense, for them. So when he has a prophetic premonition of the ruin of Monte Cassino, the monastery which he had built, Benedict, in great distress, nevertheless obtains from the Lord that the lives of the people are spared.[41] In fact, all the monks will be able to escape at the time of the Lombards' attack which will sack their monastery. Benedict's prudence reaches its peak in his sense of persons, which he wants to find in the abbot and in his principal collaborators. The Benedictine world does not simply offer a society well regulated by sufficiently strong, flexible and prudent institutions. It takes into account the dynamic of interpersonal relationships, and it is there that the most important issues concerning abbatial government are to be found. In this regard, Chapters 2 and 64 constitute a permanent source of inspiration for anyone in a position of responsibility, be it in the family, in business or in politics. They have rightly been mined for reflections on human management.

In all things, Saint Benedict is still saying to us today, look for the right measure, stick to human realities in their diversity, lead those who are in your charge with prudence and humanity.

---

[41]   *Life*, ch. 17.

Wisdom

Into a brief description of what we would call the monastery's guest house, Saint Benedict slips this general instruction: "The house of God will be administered in a wise manner by wise people".[42] Indeed, the biblical ideal of the wise man can be found throughout the *Rule*: not only the prudent man of whom we have just been speaking, but the one who has assimilated the great laws of human wisdom and who has above all been initiated into divine wisdom. "The fear of God is the beginning of wisdom" (Ps 111, 10). This is indeed the path taken by Saint Benedict himself, following the entire monastic tradition. He teaches us to live in the presence of God, in order to stir up the salutary fear and sense of mystery which prepares the soul to follow Christ along the path of obedience and humility, in order to be purified by His Holy Spirit and led to the perfection of charity. This is a fire of love which will carry us towards God and render our love of neighbour truly ardent. It thus sheds a penetrating light on human life and ultimately blossoms in a gaze full of wisdom.

The *Rule* is the fruit of Saint Benedict's wisdom, and it is no exaggeration to say that this *Rule* is one of the great texts of universal wisdom. Above all, it has guided generations of men and women towards divine wisdom, which took flesh in the person of Jesus Christ. They have studied it, practised it with fidelity and perseverance, and allowed themselves to be filled with its spirit. According to the spiritual tradition, founded on the source text of the prophet Isaiah (cf. Is 11, 1–4), both fear and wisdom are gifts of the Holy Spirit. Fear, the more humble of the two, leads to the more sublime wisdom. Both are poured out

---

[42]   RB 53, 22.

in all their fullness on the shoot of Jesse, He who is the Son
of David and the Son of Mary: Jesus.

So it is logical that Saint Gregory has described Saint
Benedict's vision of wisdom as he draws near to his death.
He receives the grace to see the whole world in the light of
God.[43] In his last meeting with his sister Scholastica, it is
the longing for Heaven which gains ascendancy. These two,
passionately in love with God, spend the night speaking of
the joys of the life of Heaven, to which they already belong
by an ever purer and stronger attraction.[44] The practical
wisdom to which the *Rule* bears witness develops into the
mystical wisdom spoken of in the *Life* of Saint Benedict.
These two kinds of wisdom are in fact only one, for in both
cases, it is the light of God which shines on created realities
and enables them to be seen in all their grandeur and
minuteness, in order to set souls on fire with the Love that
finds its source in the Heart of God. Saint Benedict's disciple
radiates this wisdom that comes from above.

Wisdom is a gift of the Spirit to which fidelity to the
Rule disposes us. Saint Benedict teaches us to see all things
in the light of divine love. This is a fruit of detachment
from self and from our spontaneous approach to the real.
It is also a consequence of our regular contact with the
Word of God. Can Christians living in the world be asked
to supplement their times of liturgical and private prayer
with at least some moments of the *lectio divina* which
occupies such a significant place in the monastic timetable? It is up to each one to see whether this is possible.
Meditating on a passage from the Gospel or another book
of the Bible or of a spiritual author instead of reading a
newspaper article or spending quite so much time on the
Internet may seem very difficult on some days, especially

---

[43]   *Life*, ch. 35.
[44]   *Life*, ch. 33.

after a long day at work or when the house is filled with family and friends. You have to read the Word in the same way that you sow seed in the ground: by opening the heart and letting the Word act at its own pace. Sometimes it provides precisely the light I was waiting for precisely in some difficult situation. More often, it penetrates into the deep layers of my spiritual memory, gently creating in me a vision of the world as God sees it, which is what we are here calling wisdom. As in other areas of the Christian and monastic life, faithfulness to a daily or weekly practice is a guarantee of fruit in our lives.

"Listen, my son, my daughter",[45] Saint Benedict is still saying to us today, to the Father's voice speaking to you and gradually introducing you into His vision of love and mercy.

Joy in Christ

Saint Benedict explicitly says that he has given elementary instructions to disciples who are ready to acknowledge that they are beginners.[46] These know that they are always on the way. They give themselves each day to the toil and joy of the Christian life. They willingly become disciples, because they know their need to be taught and guided: to be corrected, sometimes; to be stimulated often; to be constantly encouraged to believe, to hope, and above all to love.

From their first steps, however, they go forward in Christ's merciful and loving company. It is with His help that they put the instructions of the *Rule* into practice.[47] He is also the One who calls them at the appropriate hour and sets them on the infinite path of love,[48] towards the

---

[45]	Prologue 1.
[46]	RB 73, 1.
[47]	RB 73, 8.

"heights of learning and virtue ".⁴⁹ As life proceeds and becomes simpler, the gaze of their hearts falls more and more often upon the face of Christ. "To prefer nothing to the love of Christ";⁵⁰ "to have nothing dearer to them than Christ";⁵¹ "to prefer nothing whatever to Christ":⁵² these sayings express what was in Saint Benedict's own heart, his overriding love for Christ. They put into words the ardour of an ever increasing desire for God, that goes with watchful care to give the aspirations of the heart concrete expression in daily life.

It is always towards Christ that Saint Benedict's disciple returns. He finds in Him the inexhaustible mercy of which his own misery has constant need. He draws from Him the treasures of wisdom which will enlighten and ennoble his humble daily life. Under Christ's gaze life certainly does not immediately become perfect. But it is lit up by a light of hope, and, above all, it radiates a peaceful joy. Joy in Christ—our Brother, Master, Father, Saviour, Friend, Spouse, travelling Companion and merciful Judge—belongs, if he wants it, to the humblest of Saint Benedict's disciples.

The austerity, the seriousness and the gravity which characterise the *Rule* and which, in a certain way, are associated with Saint Benedict's person and the way he is represented in art, must not frighten us. Saint Benedict gathers joy in this desert where he precedes us and invites us to join him. The "joy of the Holy Spirit" is mentioned precisely in the chapter on Lent, where it is linked with the gift of self and with the desire for holy Easter.⁵³ Is there,

---

48   Cf. Prologue 49.
49   RB 73, 9.
50   RB 4, 21.
51   RB 5, 1.
52   RB 72, 11.
53   RB 49, 6–7.

then, a joy of desire? Yes, when we are sure that that desire is going to be fulfilled, because it is based on solid hope in the Father's mercy.

Dare to desire God, and life in God, Saint Benedict is still saying to us today, dare to entrust yourself completely to His infinite mercy, and enter ever more fully into the great joy of hope.

CONCLUSION: PRAISE AND COMMUNION

P UTTING ONESELF IN the school of Saint Benedict, being inspired by his spirit—or, as we say, by his spirituality—even when living in the world, is possible if we follow the advice Pope Francis expressed in a forceful and original way in his apostolic exhortation *The Joy of the Gospel* at the beginning of his pontificate. "Time," he declares there, "is greater than space".[1] Giving priority to time, means, in the Pope's words, being concerned about "initiating processes rather than possessing spaces".[2]

Following Saint Benedict, then, is not so much about building a monastery as about initiating a process of conversion which has its source in the powerful graces of our baptism and its destination in our heavenly homeland. To be sure, the enclosure of the monastery and stability in the "workshop of the spiritual craft"[3] define a "space" which is very important for monks and nuns, guaranteeing them the solitude and silence where their particular vocation can flourish. But the Benedictine "spiritual craft" cannot be reduced to the possession of a space, however precious the monastery may be as a symbol of the mystery of the union of Christ and the Church. This craft involves an evangelical process of configuration to Christ, characterised especially by divine praise and fraternal communion.

Saint Benedict's disciples over the course of the centuries have always been men and women of praise. Divine

---

[1]   Pope Francis, *Evangelii Gaudium* (2013), 222.
[2]   *Ibid.*, 223.
[3]   RB 4, 78.

praise marks the rhythm of their daily lives. They read the Word of God and study it. They pray, make supplication, implore, intercede and give thanks. In all this, they lead a life of praise, the gratuity of which is their dearest privilege. Why praise God, if not for his mercy which shines out of all his works, from the creation of the world to the Cross of Jesus and the sending of the Holy Spirit in the Church right up to the heavenly Jerusalem? The heavenly city resounds with constant praise, and monastic prayer strives to be united with this, while being fully aware of its imperfections and poverty.

But praise overflows beyond its expression in the Liturgy. Life itself becomes praise. The whole person longs to be transformed by the Spirit into "praise of God's glorious grace" (Eph 1, 3–14). Becoming acquainted with Saint Benedict leads us sooner or later to allow ourselves to be attracted to the praise which is our eternal vocation, but which is already the foundation of the Church's life. Dom Guéranger loved to define the Church as the "society of divine praise". For praise is the supreme witness, the highest form of preaching, which shows God to the world, even though it is oblivious of all that is not God and allows us to be completely fascinated by Him alone. The "Glory be to the Father, and to the Son and to the Holy Spirit..." which concludes each psalm, and for which the monk respectfully stands up and makes a deep bow out of reverence for the Blessed Trinity,[4] symbolizes the impulse to praise the thrice holy God which runs through the Church's whole life.

Living as a disciple of Saint Benedict thus consists in allowing praise to unify my life of prayer—and my entire life, full stop. This praise accompanies me from my very first steps along my spiritual path. It is, if you like, the bass

---

4   Cf. RB 9, 7.

line over which the score of my life is played out. Little by little it will attract to itself the best of what I am. I come to devote the best of my time to it, not out of any narcissistic spiritual greed, but because of a powerful impulse which sweeps up my whole soul and directs my entire life, with infinite gratitude, towards the glory of the Holy Trinity.

At the same time my life becomes unified in praise and I open myself up to an ever wider communion. The heart set free for praise by the Holy Spirit is a heart prompt to love. The pulsation of the eternal Love of the three Divine Persons becomes the rhythm of all human relationships. On the path of humility which leads to charity, the Benedictine makes himself the servant of his brethren and enters, with them, and with the whole cosmos, into a relationship of communion in the Spirit. Thus it is that I learn to allow the Holy Spirit, the eternal bond between the Father and the Son, to weave the fabric of the interior communion of the human communities to which I belong: my family, my parish, my diocese, my country, the universal Church, the whole human family. The Spirit weaves the bonds of love, friendship, brotherhood, fatherhood and sonship wherein I go forward with others, with my brothers and sisters in Christ. Thus, by His Holy Spirit who works in the hearts of His "workers" who are in the process of being purified,[5] Christ builds us up as human beings, beings in relation, made for communion, called to reflect, here below, the unity of the Trinity.

Saint Benedict's wisdom has made him a builder of human communities. It is not by chance that he was the first to be designated by Paul VI in 1964 as patron of Europe. The *Rule* articulates with finesse and perfect balance the role held by the written law, the role exercised by the living authority of the superior, and the role of each person in the building

---

[5]   Cf. RB 7, 70.

up of the community. The purpose of the order maintained by just legislation and strong authority is to arrange space and safety wherein persons can enter into relations with one another in a peaceful and lasting way, giving themselves up to the slow process of conversion of heart, in order to become open to the Holy Spirit who establishes between them the indestructible bonds of the divine life.

Once again, this magnificent path is indeed what Pope Francis called a "process", a spiritual path, a dynamic of life. Why should we be surprised, then, if this is a paschal path? We cannot follow Christ in life without taking up His cross. At the end of the Prologue, Saint Benedict tells the monk that he will be participating in Christ's Passion most especially by patience.[6] Patience is an art that requires time, a spiritual force unfolding over time. It is sometimes practised amidst considerable problems and difficulties, but is more often required when we are confronted with our inadequacies and the minute but tenacious temptations which seem to hinder the expansion of the divine life in our hearts. Patient with others, but above all with himself, Saint Benedict's disciple allows the cross of Jesus to take in his life the particular form which falls to him. With it, he passes through the valley of the shadow of death in order to enter into the light of Easter morning. For it is indeed by the path of patience that Saint Benedict leads his disciples toward largeness of heart in praise and communion.

You, then, whoever you are, who feel drawn by the Spirit to make yourself the disciple of a master as reliable as Saint Benedict, open his Rule without fear. Welcome his warm invitation to follow Christ. "Listen" to the Father's voice,[7] and walk joyfully along the path of the

---

6   Prologue 50.
7   Prologue 1.

Gospel,[8] with your heart enlarged in love,[9] overflowing with praise and charity, following in the footsteps of the Lord who brings us "all together"[10] to the home of His Father and our Father.

8   Prologue 21.
9   Prologue 48.
10   RB 72, 12.

Lightning Source UK Ltd.
Milton Keynes UK
UKHW010435040722
405291UK00001B/14